T0247884

Engineering for the Future

The Editors of *Scientific American*

SCIENTIFIC | EDUCATIONAL
AMERICAN | PUBLISHING

New York

Published in 2025 by Scientific American Educational Publishing
in association with The Rosen Publishing Group
2544 Clinton Street, Buffalo NY 14224

Contains material from Scientific American®, a division of Springer Nature America, Inc.,
reprinted by permission, as well as original material from The Rosen Publishing Group®.

First Edition

Scientific American
Lisa Pallatroni: Project Editor

Rosen Publishing
David Kuchta: Compiling Editor
Michael Moy: Senior Graphic Designer

Cataloging-in-Publication Data
Names: Scientific American, Inc.
Title: Engineering for the future / edited by the Scientific American Editors.
Description: First Edition. | New York : Scientific American Educational Publishing, 2025. |
Series: Scientific American explores big ideas | Includes bibliographical references and index.
Identifiers: ISBN 9781725351837 (pbk.) | ISBN 9781725351844
(library bound) | ISBN 9781725351851 (ebook)
Subjects: LCSH: Environmental engineering–Juvenile literature. | Green technology-
-Juvenile literature. | Sustainable engineering–Juvenile literature.
Classification: LCC TA170.E544 2025 | DDC 628–dc23

Manufactured in the United States of America
Websites listed were live at the time of publication.

Cover: maxuser/Shutterstock.com

CPSIA Compliance Information: Batch # CSSA25.
For Further Information contact Rosen Publishing at 1-800-237-9932.

CONTENTS

INTRODUCTION

From climate change and health to transportation and agriculture, engineering in all its forms will play a major role as humans face global challenges in the coming years, just as they have in the past. Since the beginning of the Industrial Revolution, engineers have had a major impact on how we live our lives. Biomedical engineers developed new medicines and medical procedures to extend our lifespans dramatically. Mechanical engineers developed combustion engines that release vast amounts of energy by burning fossil fuels. Chemical engineers learned how to draw nitrogen from the atmosphere to create fertilizers that fostered the 20th century population boom. Computer engineers brought us the Internet, smartphones, and artificial intelligence (AI).

That's the upside of engineering. The downside of the many engineering breakthroughs of the last two centuries is the threat of climate change, nuclear holocaust, overpopulation, the plague of fake news and misinformation, the ability to manipulate our genetic makeup, microplastics in the foods we eat, and the widespread extinction of species, among other threats. The engineers of the past two centuries created much of the modern world we live in. The engineers of the future will need to rise to the many challenges that the modern world has created.

In Section 1, we look at some of the engineering efforts to address climate change. Section 2 looks at the role of biotechnology in protecting the health of humans and other species. Section 3 examines how computer engineers are expanding the scope of computer power in novel and perhaps troubling ways. Section 4 looks more specifically at the key role that transportation engineers will play in helping us get around without destroying the planet, while Section 5 looks at how engineering can address the challenge of feeding an ever-growing human population.

Tinkering with how we do things always comes with opportunities and risks. In the coming years, engineers will need to get it right.

Section 1: The Climate Crisis

Entire Buildings Can Be Wrapped in Jackets to Save Energy

By Willem Marx

O n a normally peaceful residential road outside The Hague, the Dutch city that serves as seat of government, the whine of a hoisting crane and welding tools heralds a not-so-quiet housing revolution. Four workers standing above me on a scissor lift next to an apartment complex guide a thermally insulated facade 40 feet wide and one story tall into place against the existing wall. Its brickwork pattern of muted brown, grey and beige, and the triple glazed windows, perfectly fit the building's existing frame and openings.

The original windows and the very old brick walls had allowed cold drafts inside, and warm interior air to escape, wasting much of the energy used to heat the building. The new facade is primarily fire-resistant expanded polystyrene—essentially, hollow spheres that trap air to create a thick insulation layer—faced with hardened clay and sculpted into hundreds of very thin rectangles known as "brick slips."

This new building skin, prebuilt in a factory, was one of a dozen such facades to be attached to local buildings when I visited the suburb on a rainy day in early summer, each structure measured to millimeter precision. The installation is part of a concerted effort to transform energy-inefficient public housing into a set of ultralow-emission homes—without having to open a wall or remake an attic. The building was being wrapped in the equivalent of a winter jacket— or summer beer koozie—avoiding the need to insert insulation inside dozens of walls, lofts and attics. A similarly premade, lightweight, highly insulating material, complete with solar panels, would be installed on the roof, too.

In developed economies like the Netherlands and the United States, a big chunk of greenhouse gas emissions can be attributed to energy loss in residential buildings. But retrofitting homes to improve efficiency and reduce carbon footprint too often remains cumbersome and costly. The work requires a constellation of contractors and up-front financing that is off-putting for homeowners and landlords, despite the long-term environmental and financial benefits.

The Dutch government began to confront this climate challenge a decade ago by seed-funding a nonprofit program known as Energiesprong, or "energy leap" in Dutch. The initial investment helped bring together engineers, construction companies, hardware suppliers, financiers, regulators and landlords who figured out a way to mass-produce home retrofits.

Landlords planning a routine refurbishment of their housing stock can now simply add an energy retrofit to that process, with attractive new facades and roofs. An automated laser device takes precision measurements of a building's entire exterior in a matter of hours. The information is uploaded wirelessly to large factories where walls, windows, doors and solar roofs are mass-produced and fit together for the target building. Completed facades and roofs are trucked to the site and attached. Often, the building owner or residents see their annual energy costs fall to zero thanks to solar panels that sell excess power to the national grid, at least during the summer.

The average retrofit cost in the Netherlands is about $94,000 for a family home, typically a row house. That may sound high, but it is comparable to the cost of other routine renovations that deliver no energy savings. In one neighborhood in the city of Utrecht, more than a dozen houses and some 250 separate apartments retrofitted in 2019 saw their energy requirements fall from 225 kilowatt-hours per square meter to just 50 kilowatt-hours per square meter, on average. The remaining demand for energy was met with solar power.

These steep energy savings are prompting owners to sign up for retrofits without any public financing (although a solar subsidy is available). And other countries and communities are modeling new programs on the Energiesprong approach. Recently, the New

York State Energy Research and Development Authority directed $30 million to its own program, called RetrofitNY.

The facades being installed in The Hague had been manufactured by RC Panels, a vendor two hours east of the city in Lemelerveld. The for-profit company is focused on insulating the country's more than two million row houses and many more apartment dwellings. Lianda Sjerps-Koomen, the firm's business development manager, walks me through a factory floor the size of an aircraft hangar, pointing out teams of workers pulling together the various layers of raw materials for a wall facade. Powerful vacuum cranes glom on to the panels, ushering them along an assembly line until a vast cutting machine slices out precisely measured window and door holes from the huge sheets of the expanded polystyrene and other layers.

"We need millions of houses to be renovated for the energy transition," Sjerps-Koomen says, as nearby camera-operated twin robot arms stamp six brick slips per second into one of the facades passing horizontally beneath them. The factory makes retrofits for hundreds of homes across the country each year, just as factories mass-produce cars or kitchen counters—an approach the housing retrofit industry is just not accustomed to, Sjerps-Koomen tells me.

At Factory Zero, another Dutch enterprise, engineers have designed a single rooftop module that houses an electric boiler for hot water, heat pump to warm the home, a smart meter and a solar power hookup. These units are often a major part of an energy retrofit, but are usually done piecemeal, by different contractors or trades, and typically require custom, costly installation. Just days after an order comes in to Factory Zero, the firm's installation teams can crane-drop a completed module onto the top of a flat- or pitched-roofed home, or next to one.

The company is making about 1,000 modules a year, and it charges around $16,000 per installation. It claims the typical cost in the Netherlands might be $35,000 if several different suppliers were working separately. As more homes are retrofitted, costs should come down. That change might allow many more large landlords, such as local governments, to finance the retrofit work as part of their regular property maintenance.

"We're trying to get the price of a modern energy system down to a level where it's affordable for everybody," says Jasper van den Munckhof, one of the company's co-founders. But he acknowledges that mass retrofitting will have to expand dramatically if government emissions targets for 2050 are to be met. The Netherlands needs "to do a thousand net-zero retrofits a day," he explains. "Currently, we're running at 10."

Mass production is crucial for this novel industry to expand, according to Donal Brown, a British academic who directs the Sustainable Design Collective and who co-authored a recent study of Energiesprong's applicability in the United Kingdom and other markets. He describes Energiesprong as a radical business model that requires retrofit innovations and support from policy makers. For example, Brown says Dutch power suppliers allowed electricity generated by panels to feed back into their grid system during the summer, in return for homeowner credit. Without that kind of "feed-in" or "net metering" tariff in place, in the winter those homes will have to pay for any energy use. Furthermore, he says, mass retrofits only become affordable if they are done on a large scale. Without rolling out thousands of modules at a time, costs cannot halve to the level he thinks is necessary—below around $50,000 per dwelling.

In the U.S., retrofitting progress is even slower. Although some states offer incentives or rebates to homeowners who make energy-based upgrades, this house-by-house approach, implemented with an array of different contractors and suppliers, is slow, and is not making much of a dent in residential emissions.

In New York state, the energy research authority used some of its $30 million investment in RetrofitNY to initiate a contest that selects specific affordable-housing properties for retrofits. Businesses were challenged to design, build and install an appropriate retrofit, with targets for tenant comfort, cost effectiveness, style and energy performance.

Authority CEO Doreen Harris says she wants to be a "catalyst" for the broader investments needed to retrofit the current housing sector, by demonstrating that mass-produced technologies and approaches work. Her team recently allocated $1.8 million to a $20 million retrofit project for nine buildings, containing 146 apartments, in the Bushwick neighborhood of Brooklyn. The nonprofit owner of the complex estimates the overhaul will reduce long-term energy use by 80 percent, and cut its annual costs by $180,000, once the final phase is completed later this year. If that project succeeds, polystyrene facades being hoisted onto the sides of large apartment buildings may become a more common sight.

About the Author

Willem Marx is a magazine, radio and television journalist based in London.

New Air-Conditioning Technology Could Be the Future of Cool

By Lauren Leffer

J uly 2023 was the hottest recorded month in human history. Heat waves smashed temperature records worldwide and even brought summer temperatures to Chile and Argentina during the Southern Hemisphere's winter. It's more than just a matter of sweaty discomfort. Severe heat is the deadliest of all weather events; in the U.S. alone, it kills more people each year than floods, tornadoes and hurricanes combined. As climate change worsens, access to artificially cooled spaces is rapidly becoming a health necessity—and an issue of basic human rights.

Yet standard air-conditioning systems have ensnared us in a negative feedback loop: the hotter it is, the more people crank the AC—and the more energy is used (and greenhouse gases are emitted) as a result. "We're in a vicious cycle," says Nicole Miranda, an engineer researching sustainable cooling at the University of Oxford. And "it's not only a vicious cycle, but it's an accelerating one." Cooling is the fastest-growing single source of energy use in buildings, according to 2018 data from the International Energy Agency (IEA). Following a business-as-usual scenario, the IEA projects that worldwide annual energy demand from cooling will more than triple by 2050. That's an increase of more than 4,000 terawatt-hours, which is about how much energy the entire U.S. uses in a year.

It's becoming increasingly clear that humans cannot outrun climate change with the same air-conditioning technology we've been using for nearly a century. Breaking the cycle requires new innovations that will help bring cooler air to more people with less environmental impact.

One well-known problem with current AC systems is their reliance on refrigerant chemicals, many of which are potent greenhouse gases.

Some projects aim to replace these substances with less-harmful coolants—but even if they do, the refrigerants make up only a fraction of air-conditioning's climate toll. About 80 percent of a standard AC unit's climate-warming emissions currently come from the energy used to power it, says Nihar Shah, director of the Global Cooling Efficiency Program at Lawrence Berkeley National Laboratory. A lot of recent work has gone into boosting the energy efficiency of compressors and heat exchangers, which are parts of standard AC designs, Shah explains. Yet more ambitious projects aim to reduce the amount of work those components must do in the first place.

Standard air-conditioning systems simultaneously cool and dehumidify through a relatively inefficient mechanism: in order to condense water out of the air, Shah says, they overcool that air past the point of comfort. Many new designs therefore separate the dehumidification and cooling processes, which avoids the need to overcool.

For example, some newer air conditioner designs pull moisture from the air with desiccant materials (similar to the silica gel in the packets you might find in a bag of jerky or a bottle of pills). The dried air can then be cooled to a more reasonable temperature. This process can require some additional energy because the desiccant needs to be "recharged" using heat. But some companies, including the Somerville, Mass.–based start-up Transaera, recycle the heat generated by the cooling process to recharge the desiccant. Transaera claims that the system it is developing could use 35 percent less energy than the average standard AC unit.

Even bigger efficiency gains are possible when dehumidification is paired with evaporative cooling, which takes the energy-intensive process called vapor compression out of the equation altogether. Vapor compression—the system by which standard AC works—moves a refrigerant through a cycle in which it is variably condensed and expanded, enabling it to absorb heat from inside and release that heat outside. Conversely, evaporative cooling is a simpler process. It's the same one through which sweating cools our skin: as water goes from liquid to gas, it absorbs heat. Swamp coolers, DIY devices in which a fan blows air over ice, work the same way. And in dry climates, people have used evaporative cooling for thousands of years. In ancient Iran, for instance, people engineered *yakhchāls*—large, cone-shaped clay structures with solar chimneys—which harnessed air circulation and the evaporation of adjacent water to lower temperatures so much that they could make ice in winter and store it through summer.

But this strategy also increases air's humidity, so as a cooling system, it tends to work only when the weather is hot and dry; if humidity rises beyond a certain point, it cancels out the comfort gains of reduced temperature. To solve this, research groups, including Harvard University's cSNAP team, have designed AC devices that use a hydrophobic barrier to perform evaporative cooling while holding back humidity. As a bonus, refrigerants—which are often greenhouse gases that are many times more potent than carbon dioxide—aren't involved at all. "We expect to provide a 75 percent more energy-efficient air conditioner," says Jonathan Grinham, an assistant professor of architecture at Harvard and one of cSNAP's lead designers.

Meanwhile Florida-based company Blue Frontier is trialing a commercial air-conditioning system based on both a desiccant (in this case, a liquid salt solution) and evaporative cooling. This design dries the air and then splits it into two adjacent streams, explains the company's CEO, Daniel Betts. The air in one stream is directly cooled through the reintroduction of moisture and evaporation. The other airstream is kept dry, and it is cooled by being run across a thin aluminum wall that pulls in the cold—but not the humidity—from the first stream. The liquid salt desiccant then runs through a heat pump system to be recharged. To maximize efficiency, the heat pump can be run at night, when the power grid is least stressed, and the desiccant can then be stored for use in the hottest part of the day. Based on the company's field trials, "we're looking at 50 to 90 percent reductions in energy consumption," Betts claims.

But Blue Frontier, cSNAP and Transaera have yet to go from testing to market. All three groups predict they're at least a couple of years away from commercial launch. And even then, there will be obstacles that could prevent the new systems from replacing traditional ACs. These include relatively higher manufacturing and installation costs, industry inertia and policies that incentivize cheap systems over efficient ones.

Even with some of the best technologies available, the gains in efficiency alone might not be enough to offset the widely expected uptick in air-conditioning use. Under the best-case model, the IEA projects that cooling worldwide will require 50 percent more energy in the next 25 years than it does now because of rising demand, Shah says. It will not work to simply replace every existing air conditioner with a better model and call it a day. Instead a truly cooler future will have to employ other, passive strategies that rely on urban planning and building design to minimize the need for cooling in the first place. Bringing greenery and water bodies into cityscapes, shading windows, positioning new buildings to take advantage of natural airflow and retrofitting buildings with better insulation and reflective panels that can send heat into space are all critical, both Shah and Miranda say.

"Cooling is a multi-faceted challenge," says Sneha Sachar, an energy efficiency expert at the nonprofit organization ClimateWorks. "There isn't one strategy or one answer." We need a combination of better buildings and cities, better technology and a better understanding that the true cost of air-conditioning extends beyond electric bills. "What we do in one part of the world impacts the whole global environment," Sachar says.

About the Author

Lauren Leffer is a contributing writer and former tech reporting fellow at Scientific American. *She reports on many subjects including artificial intelligence, climate and weird biology because she's curious to a fault. When she's not writing, she's hopefully hiking. Follow her on X (formerly Twitter) @lauren_leffer and on Bluesky @laurenleffer.bsky.social.*

Recycled Wind Turbines Could Be Made into Plexiglass, Diapers or Gummy Bears

By Sophie Bushwick

The blades of a wind turbine are typically designed to be replaced about every 20 years. This means that, as wind energy becomes more popular, more and more of these hulking fiberglass structures will be discarded, and many of them could end up buried in the ground. To encourage recycling the blades instead, one research team has developed a binding resin—the ingredient that holds their fibrous material together—that can be transformed into more valuable substances.

"We've specifically designed a system with the end of life in mind," says John Dorgan, a professor of chemical engineering and materials science at Michigan State University, who worked on developing the new resin. After being used for years to strengthen wind turbine blades or other structures, the resin can be recycled back into another turbine blade or downcycled into a composite material that can be used to make plastic products. It can also be processed to produce more valuable chemicals: these upcycled options include the shatter-resistant acrylic plexiglass, a superabsorbent polymer used in diapers and the food preservative potassium lactate—which Dorgan used to make gummy bears that he then ate.

Wind turbine blades are typically 170 feet long, roughly the length of an Olympic-sized swimming pool. But because bigger turbines can capture more energy, some offshore wind farms are investing in taller installations that can sport blades nearly twice as long. When these massive blades are damaged or reach the end of their lifetime, they must be retired from use. By 2050, experts estimate that more than two million tons of blade material could be decommissioned each year.

There are two main obstacles to recycling these structures. "To start with is just the fact that they're very large, and they're meant to be very durable—to last in the weather for 20 or more years. So they're just a hard thing to disassemble and move around," explains Aubryn Cooperman, a wind energy analyst at the National Renewable Energy Laboratory, who was not involved in the new resin's development. Another problem "is that they're made from materials that are as low-cost as possible [that will] still get the performance you need." For maximum efficiency, wind turbine blades must be both light and strong, so engineers typically craft them from fiberglass bonded together with a polymer resin. In theory, this material can be recycled, but researchers say the resulting product is not particularly valuable. "The main problem is: it's simply uneconomic to do it," Dorgan says. "It's cheaper to just bury it in the ground than it is to reprocess it into something useful."

To solve this problem, recycling wind turbine blades must become easier and more profitable. Several companies in the renewable energy industry—including Siemens Gamesa, General Electric and Vestas—are working on this issue, Cooperman says. "Anything that makes it easy to recycle, that makes it less costly to recycle, increases the chances of more recycling happening," she notes.

Dorgan and his colleagues decided to develop a new polymer resin that could bind a large fiberglass structure firmly together while it is in use and that could be turned into a variety of products when the time comes to retire the blade. The team produced a syrupy resin by dissolving polylactide, a polymer derived from plants, in a synthetic monomer called methyl methacrylate (MMA). Next, the researchers used vacuum pressure to pull the resin through glass fibers. After the fibers had been impregnated with the liquid, the resin hardened, producing solid fiberglass panels. The same process can be used to make larger structures, including wind turbine blades and boat hulls. The team presented the work this week at a meeting of the American Chemical Society.

When the time came to recycle their experimental fiberglass panels, the researchers had a few options. In one, they could crush up the panels and add an additional polymer, producing a plastic material that could be transformed into other objects through injection molding. This short-fiber composite might become the basis of computer housings or other objects but would not be particularly valuable, Dorgan says. Another option was to make strong new panels from the remains of the old ones:

the team soaked the panels in the MMA monomer, which dissolved the hardened resin—then the researchers physically removed the glass fibers. The recovered "syrup" was used to make fresh fiberglass panels, which had the same physical properties as the originals.

But the leftover resin also has other potential uses. "What would really drive recycling of wind turbines is if you could turn them into something that's worth more money or by using it to [make high-value] products out of it," Dorgan says. For instance, putting the recovered resin through different chemical reactions allowed the team to extract new compounds. One substance produced this way was polymethyl methacrylate, an acrylic polymer better known as plexiglass. This transparent, shatter-proof substance is valued as an alternative to glass in a vast variety of goods, ranging from windows to car headlights. Cooking the resin at a high temperature produced poly(methacrylic acid), a superabsorbent material used in diapers and other products. A little more processing resulted in potassium lactate, which is added to a variety of foods as a preservative. Although Dorgan did use it to make his own version of gummy bears, he does not necessarily see homemade candy as the primary way to improve the recyclability of wind turbine blades. His goal is to encourage recycling by changing attitudes.

"I'm trying to push the boundaries of how people think about recycling," he explains. "It's about creating additional options and getting people to think about 'What really are the limits on recycling?' And as far as I know, nobody's ever reprocessed a durable composite material into something that can be eaten."

About the Author

Sophie Bushwick is tech editor at Scientific American. *She runs the daily technology news coverage for the website, writes about everything from artificial intelligence to jumping robots for both digital and print publication, records YouTube and TikTok videos and hosts the podcast* Tech, Quickly. *Bushwick also makes frequent appearances on radio shows such as* Science Friday *and television networks, including CBS, MSNBC and National Geographic. She has more than a decade of experience as a science journalist based in New York City and previously worked at outlets such as* Popular Science, Discover *and* Gizmodo. *Follow Bushwick on X (formerly Twitter)* @sophiebushwick.

New Space Station Sensor Can Reveal Hidden Greenhouse Gas Polluters

By Meghan Bartels

An instrument recently installed on the International Space Station (ISS) is proving its mettle at spotting plumes of greenhouse gases that are altering Earth's climate.

The sensor, called Earth Surface Mineral Dust Source Investigation (EMIT), was delivered to the space station in the summer of 2022. Its main purpose is to determine how dust in the atmosphere affects Earth's climate. But it turns out this capability also enables EMIT to gather highly detailed observations of previously unknown plumes of the key greenhouse gases methane and carbon dioxide, according to new research that analyzed the instrument's first 30 days of data. Scientists hope the ability to pinpoint emission sources can be a valuable tool in tackling the climate crisis as greenhouse gases reach ever higher concentrations in the atmosphere, as announced by the World Meteorological Organization in November 2023.

The EMIT sensor is so valuable because it pairs the precision of technology such as airplane-mounted instruments with the wide coverage of satellites.

"With a lot of the previous methods, you might get a sense of what's happening in a broad region or a city, but it's not always possible to attribute the emissions to, let's say, this part of the city, this power plant, this landfill," says John Lin, an atmospheric scientist at the University of Utah, who was not involved in the new study, published in *Science Advances*. "That type of attribution becomes quite useful, especially if we think about ways to reduce these emissions."

EMIT has already spent more than a year watching Earth. These observations have prioritized monitoring dust, however—so the instrument has so far focused on particularly dusty regions such as northern Africa and Central Asia. As a secondary task, greenhouse gas sensing overall has taken a back seat; in the scant time available to date for emissions work, the team has prioritized studying methane over carbon dioxide because methane sources aren't as well understood, according to mission personnel. That might change if NASA continues the mission into 2024 and beyond, says EMIT's principal investigator Robert Green, an Earth systems scientist at NASA's Jet Propulsion Laboratory (JPL) and a co-author of the study.

But the paper outlines how, even in just its first month of dust-focused observations, EMIT also identified dozens of different methane plumes, as well as carbon dioxide emissions from such as two Chinese power plants and a Saudi Arabian landfill.

The results aren't completely unexpected—EMIT team members had thought they would be able to see greenhouse gases with the instrument. The quality of its performance, even in its initial work, came as a surprise, however, says Andrew Thorpe, a technologist and atmospheric scientist at JPL and lead author of the new study. "We were ecstatic when we saw the results, and we're very excited about the performance of the instrument," he says. "It exceeded our expectations."

These results put EMIT in a wave of next-generation space-based sensors that are looking for greenhouse gas plumes—including an already flying satellite from Montreal-based company GHGSat, as well as future missions from the nonprofits Carbon Mapper and Environmental Defense Fund—says Lori Bruhwiler, an atmospheric scientist at the National Oceanic and Atmospheric Administration's Global Monitoring Laboratory, who was not involved in the new research. "We need as much data as we can get," she says, "so the fact that there are multiple instruments up there doing this sort of thing, it's a good thing."

The new tools are important because of high-resolution observations that mimic the quality of measurements that are typically made by airplanes. But EMIT's perch on the ISS allows it to cover much more ground than any plane. It combines powerful technologies for identifying sources of emissions that might easily be addressed, scientists say—particularly for pipelines, the owners of which have economic motivation to plug leaks.

"If you can really home in on what's happening and measure it from space with large coverage, then you can really provide a lot of information to see some of the low-hanging fruit, some of the large sources we can go after," Lin says.

Although the new research covers only 30 days of observations, Green says that EMIT has observed more than 830 greenhouse gas plumes to date. The EMIT team is posting its data publicly and says some voluntary emissions reduction measures have already been taken because of its work—although the researchers don't reach out to the creators of plumes they detect. "Science can give you this information," Bruhwiler says. "But then the action, that requires policy and diplomacy."

In the new research, the team members also attempt to quantify the emissions they observed. This can inform officials' inventories of greenhouse gas emissions, which are formal tallies of sources and sinks. (The latter include trees that take up carbon dioxide.) Bruhwiler cautions that these calculations require a detailed understanding of local atmospheric conditions, which isn't feasible for places with weaker weather-monitoring infrastructure.

Even if EMIT is limited in its ability to inventory greenhouse gases, its data could still help countries meet 2021's global methane-reduction pledge, which aims to reduce emissions by at least 30 percent of 2020's levels by 2030. Methane is a more powerful greenhouse gas on a per-molecule basis than carbon dioxide and is also shorter-lived in the atmosphere, making it an appealing target for short-term action. "If we could really reduce methane emissions, we could reduce the rate of warming in the next few decades," Lin says.

Nearly 150 nations and regions have signed the methane-reduction pledge. Yet its ambitious target will require the world to make real strides in reducing emissions—including from tough-to-cut sources such as livestock facilities—rather than simply patching leaks in power infrastructure, Bruhwiler says. "The fact is that we're not going to be able to meet the global methane pledge with just oil and gas emissions," she says. "That's the low-hanging fruit, the thing that we know to fix, the thing we know we can fix without too much economic pain. But in the end, it's not going to be enough."

The more tools scientists can use to identify greenhouse gas plumes, the more targets are available to reduce emissions—not only in the context of the methane pledge but also in terms of climate change targets established by the United Nations. The world body is set to hold its 28th annual Climate Change Conference, also called the 28th Conference of the Parties to the U.N. Framework Convention on Climate Change (COP28), later this month in the United Arab Emirates. At COP28, nations will especially be focusing on carbon dioxide emissions, which the EMIT team will also be targeting next.

"Eventually we have to tackle CO_2—and the CO_2 part of the problem is rapidly growing and not showing any signs of slowing down right now," Bruhwiler says. "We should definitely mitigate methane emissions, no doubt about it. We can benefit from that. But somewhere down the line we're going to have to seriously confront CO_2."

About the Author

Meghan Bartels is a science journalist based in New York City. She joined Scientific American *in 2023 and is now a senior news reporter. Previously, she spent more than four years as a writer and editor at* Space.com, *as well as nearly a year as a science reporter at* Newsweek, *where she focused on space and Earth science. Her writing has also appeared in* Audubon, Nautilus, Astronomy *and* Smithsonian, *among other publications. She attended Georgetown University and earned a master's in journalism at New York University's Science, Health and Environmental Reporting Program.*

Pipelines Touted as Carbon Capture Solution Spark Uncertainty and Opposition

By Anna Mattson

One hot hot summer day in 2021, Kathy Stockdale checked her mailbox and found a slip of paper that would change her life. The humble notice revealed that two carbon capture companies wanted to seize part of her family's farmland in Hardin County, Iowa, for a pair of pipelines slated to pass through it. But Stockdale wasn't going to give up her property without a fight.

Pipelines are hardly new to the Midwest; thousands of miles of natural gas conduits already crisscross the region. But fresh tension surrounds the construction of a relatively new kind of conduit called a carbon capture pipeline, and the Stockdales' land lies in the potential pathway of two of them. These pipelines are part of an effort to reduce greenhouse gas emissions from ethanol production plants by capturing and storing carbon dioxide that would otherwise be released into the atmosphere. But despite the green intentions behind the technology, environmentalists are actually joining landowners in pushing back against it. Many experts worry the pipelines could spring deadly leaks or contaminate water—and they question how effective such projects will actually be at fighting climate change.

Stockdale and her husband, Raymond, who have lived on their farm for 47 years, were stunned when representatives from a carbon capture company suddenly showed up just three months after the couple received the notice. Without asking permission, the reps began planting stakes where the pipe would go, Stockdale says. "I have never felt more disrespect in my life," she adds. She decided to fight back against the use of eminent domain—a legal concept that allows companies to seize private property for public use through the local, state or federal government (although the landowner must be fairly compensated). Stockdale has been fervently attending public hearings on permits, researching pipeline safety and talking with legislators. She has had a lot of sleepless nights. And even though she says she isn't interested in environmental protection, she has partnered with the local Sierra Club chapter for support.

Environmentalists might not seem like a natural ally in a battle against green technology, but they have concerns about the growing U.S. web of carbon capture pipelines—which currently includes more than 5,300 miles of conduit. And carbon capture technology continues to gain traction nationwide; the Biden administration recently announced that it would spend up to $1.2 billion on carbon capture and storage projects, signaling a commitment to this technology as a means to achieve net zero emissions.

Here's how the carbon capture process works: It begins at an industrial site, such as an ethanol or power plant, that produces a lot of carbon dioxide emissions. As the plant burns fossil fuels, a liquid solvent absorbs the exhaust and separates its gases. A storage chamber collects separated carbon dioxide (which would otherwise enter the atmosphere and trap heat), and harmless nitrogen and oxygen are released. Next, the system liquifies the CO_2, which flows through steel pipelines to a designated storage site. Once it arrives, another pipe injects it deep underground, where it is isolated from the atmosphere and will no longer actively contribute to climate change.

But the process comes with risks. CO_2 remains a liquid in the high-pressure, high-temperature environment inside a pipeline. But if the pipeline ruptures, that liquid escapes as a colorless, odorless gas that is difficult for people to detect without specialized instruments. This CO_2 can displace oxygen and potentially cause suffocation, drowsiness and sometimes death; in fact, the gas is sometimes pumped into specialized chambers to euthanize livestock on farms. In 2020 heavy rains triggered a landslide that damaged a carbon capture pipeline in Satartia, Miss. The pipe burst and released CO_2, suffocating 45 people so severely that they needed to be hospitalized.

Fortunately, these pipelines have a low probability of failure. Leaks are few and far between. But Bill Caram, executive director of Pipeline Safety Trust, says that any one rupture can have unacceptable consequences. "We have a goal of zero incidents. And I think that's a shared goal among regulators and the industry," Caram says. "We're a long way away from that happening."

A study released in May found that carbon capture pipelines are more likely to experience small punctures than large ruptures such as the one in Satartia. Smaller holes release the gas at a slower rate, which makes them harder to locate. And a delayed response to smaller punctures could cause them to be deadly.

When CO_2 vaporizes and escapes, it causes the temperature in the pipeline to drop immediately—a process Caram describes as "violent." The escaped gas doesn't ignite or dissipate. It moves quickly along the ground and can collect in low-lying areas, including small valleys and basements near the pipeline route. If a person in one of these pockets breathes air with a 10 percent concentration of CO_2, they can fall unconscious within one minute.

Additionally, impurities in the liquified gas can erode a pipeline and increase the chance of a leak. Potentially dangerous contaminants include water, nitrogen oxides and sulfur oxides—all of which are sometimes found in CO_2 captured from power plants. There is only limited research on how these contaminants will affect the gas's stability in storage. Experts note that relatively large concentrations of oxygen could potentially dissolve caprock, a natural geological formation that traps oil and coal—and injected CO_2—and keeps them from escaping to the surface. One of the main problems, Caram says, is that there are no federal regulations from the Pipeline and Hazardous Materials Safety Administration about limiting impurities, even after the 2020 Satartia incident. "Operators can clean it up somewhat. They can dry it out and get the water out of there to a certain extent," Caram says. "But there's no regulation saying that the pipeline can't have these impurities in it. It's just kind of up to operators to do it."

Beyond their safety concerns, experts question whether carbon capture and storage is even an effective strategy for reducing greenhouse gases. Noah Planavsky, an isotope geochemist at Yale University's Center for Natural Carbon Capture, says the practice would certainly reduce the CO_2 in the air—but the overall situation is not that simple. "It's not whether or not it'll remove carbon. It *will* remove carbon," Planavsky says. "But are we doing things that are actually propagating further use of fossil fuels?"

Investing massive amounts of money in carbon capture and storage, and the pipelines that come with it, will lower carbon dioxide levels in the atmosphere. But with limited federal money allocated for long-term climate change mitigation, Planavsky is not sure this technology is the best use of those funds. He says it's important to consider whether carbon capture will be used as an excuse for not phasing out fossil fuels.

Carbon dioxide removal, Planavsky explains, is not meant to replace emissions reduction. Instead meeting the goal of producing net-zero CO_2 emissions will require a range of solutions, including both industrial and natural carbon capture. The latter could mean preserving natural spaces such as forests, oceans, grasslands and wetlands, which naturally pull carbon dioxide from the air. Natural forms of carbon capture provide cleaner water and air, as well as increased biodiversity—things that might serve the land, rather than put holes in it.

But as more federal money goes into carbon capture pipelines and other projects, public permit hearings such as those happening in the Midwest will continue. The situation is keeping landowners, experts and locals on their toes. And until the carbon capture companies are denied building permits in Iowa, Stockdale says she will continue fighting to keep the pipelines off her land.

"It's not what I planned on doing at 72 years old. I have five grandkids who I can spend more time with," Stockdale says. "But I'm fighting for their futures."

About the Author

Anna Mattson is a freelance science journalist based in South Dakota. You can find more of her work at annamattson.com or follow her on X (formerly Twitter) @AnnaMattson9.

How to Make Urban Agriculture More Climate-Friendly

By Joanna Thompson

S troll through any trendy neighborhood of Brooklyn, N.Y., and you'll notice little pockets of green tucked between the concrete and brownstones. Many of these miniature oases are community gardens, spaces dedicated to growing produce ranging from kale to squash to tomatoes right in the heart of the city. Such projects are often seen as a climate solution—a way to enjoy fresh, local food with minimal environmental impact. But though these spaces have many upsides, reducing carbon emissions isn't always one of them.

A 2024 study in *Nature Cities* compared carbon emissions from small farms and gardens in major cities across the U.S. and Europe with those of a typical industrial farm. The results may surprise many climate-conscious and well-meaning urbanites: per serving of produce, the carbon cost of low-tech urban farms can be up to six times greater than that of industrial farming operations. "We knew it would be high, but we didn't realize it would be *so* high," says study co-author Joshua Newell, a sustainable development researcher at the University of Michigan.

But the process of growing food in cities doesn't have to be so carbon-intensive, however, Newell says. In fact, when done right, it could have huge environmental and societal benefits— and many researchers still see it as an important part of a more sustainable future.

Urban agriculture—whether it describes towering, high-tech vertical gardens or a small patch of dirt with a few basil plants—has become increasingly popular around the world as food movements such as eating local produce and growing organic crops have gained momentum. These operations are often viewed as a sustainable, community-focused alternative to big industrial farms. But until recently, few studies actually looked at their environmental impact.

Newell and his team decided it was time to change that. Using data from 73 low-tech city farms, community gardens and personal plots of land, they measured the average carbon emissions from growing a single serving of urban produce (say, one medium potato) against the carbon released by growing the equivalent on a conventional commercial farm. The team found that because of urban gardens' relatively low yields, along with the energy used in constructing the planting beds, big-city spuds were significantly more carbon-intensive than commercially grown ones. This held true even when the researchers factored in emissions from transporting commercially grown produce to often distant grocery stores. "Just because it's local doesn't mean it has a lower carbon footprint," Newell says.

One person who wasn't surprised by these results was Carolyn Dimitri, a New York University applied economist, who studies food systems but wasn't involved with the new work. Small, scattered urban plots can't compete with industrial farms in terms of output, she says. Proportionally, it takes a lot more fertilizer, water and new infrastructure to grow a serving of vegetables in a relatively tiny urban space, compared with a conventional farm, which is already designed for high yields. That massive difference in scale and optimization accounts for most of the carbon discrepancies.

That doesn't mean that growing vegetables in big cities is inherently bad, however. "Urban farming is great," if imperfect, says Carola Grebitus, a sociologist specializing in food choice at Arizona State University. It can be a powerful tool for education and job creation, she says, and a good way to introduce fresh produce to urban "food deserts" where healthy fruits and vegetables are hard to come by. Community gardens can also provide a psychologically beneficial place to connect with nature, and the added green space can help mitigate dangerous heat and flooding.

Conscious of these benefits, Newell's team highlighted a number of ways to make urban agriculture more sustainable from a climate perspective. One option is to be selective about what crops are grown. Tomatoes grown in the city, for instance, have a carbon footprint equal to or lower than their industrially farmed counterparts. That's because most commercially produced tomatoes start life in the greenhouse—a resource- and energy-intensive farming method. And a few other highly perishable crops that need to be refrigerated right away, such as asparagus and herbs, have about the same carbon footprint whether they're grown in urban or industrial farm settings.

Another strategy is to rely on existing infrastructure as much as possible. Nearly two thirds of the carbon emissions from urban agriculture came from operations related to infrastructure, including the demolition and remodeling of old buildings rather than the incorporation of these structures into a new garden's design. The equipment needed to demolish an old building, not to mention a building's original construction, can emit a lot of carbon. Finally, Newell says, any urban farm should take the local climate, water quality and soil into account. Growing plants that are ill-suited to an area requires more water, energy and pesticides, all of which take an environmental toll. Oranges won't thrive in New York City, for example, but they can bear lots of fruit under the hot Phoenix sun.

For Dimitri, this study represents an important step in opening up a more nuanced discussion about urban agriculture. She hopes that future research will highlight even more of the distinctions between commercial farms and urban gardens in different locations. "A farm in Germany is not the same as a farm in the U.S.," she says. "So it would be nice to see maybe country-by-country discussions."

Rather than a one-size-fits-all climate solution, perhaps it is best to view urban farming as something as unique as the vibrant metropolises it is practiced in—each plot as different from others as Munich is from Detroit or New York City is from Paris.

About the Author

Joanna Thompson is an insect enthusiast and former Scientific American *intern. She is based in New York City. Follow Thompson on X (formerly Twitter) @ jojofoshosho0.*

Don't Fall for Big Oil's Carbon Capture Deceptions

By Jonathan Foley

I t's that time of year again. The political and media circus of the United Nation's big climate change meeting COP 28 is about to begin, this time in 2023 in Dubai. And it's bound to be quite a show.

In the inevitable crescendo of hype and greenwashing that's coming our way, we'll doubtless hear a lot about industrial carbon capture technologies that attempt to remove carbon dioxide from the atmosphere. The COP 28 host country, the United Arab Emirates, the world's largest oil companies and even programs in the U.S. Department of Energy are working hard to push this stuff.

Don't be fooled. It's mostly a distraction from what we really need to do right now: phase out fossil fuels and deploy more effective climate solutions.

Industrial carbon capture technologies come in many flavors, but the most prominent are carbon capture and storage (CCS), which removes carbon dioxide from highly concentrated point sources like power plants, and direct air capture (DAC), which attempts to remove CO_2 from open air, where concentrations are much lower.

At first blush, this sounds great. But, as I've written previously, counting on these technologies today is a bad idea. First, industrial carbon capture projects are far too small to matter. Even after decades of investment, research and development, today's largest carbon capture projects only remove a few seconds' worth of our yearly greenhouse gas emissions. And even the planned Regional Direct Air Capture Hubs the Department of Energy is supporting will only be able to capture one million metric tonnes of CO_2 every year; last year, the world emitted 40.5 billion.

Second, they are far too expensive, costing thousands of dollars for every ton of CO_2 removed. Other climate solutions, including improving energy efficiency, deploying renewable energy sources and addressing emissions in agriculture and industrial sectors, are far more cost-effective. Industrial carbon removal costs at least $1,000 per tonne removed; many other climate solutions either have costs lower than $10 per ton, and some have negative costs, saving money immediately.

Third, these industrial carbon removal techniques also consume excessive amounts of energy, which present enormous challenges to scalability. If we power carbon capture projects with CO_2-spewing fossil fuels, the projects lose much of their proposed climate benefit. Moreover, powering them with renewable or nuclear energy sources would provide far less climate benefit than using that energy to directly displace fossil fuels.

In addition, CO_2 captured by industrial carbon capture projects is often used to drive more oil and gas back out—for something known as enhanced oil recovery, which uses fluids like carbon dioxide to push oil and gas out of rock formations—helping fossil fuel companies continue working.

Industrial carbon capture also does nothing to reduce the health damage caused by fossil fuels. Most notably, sucking CO_2 out of the air fails to relieve the tremendous air pollution effects of burning fossil fuels, which cause 8–9 million people to die prematurely each year.

More fundamentally, the biggest problem with industrial carbon capture schemes is that they are largely a ploy by Big Oil to delay action to phase out fossil fuels.

These projects give fossil fuel companies a greenwashing boost, cloaking pollution underneath fake environmental responsibility, helping them claim that they are taking serious climate action, all the while continuing to build out additional fossil fuel infrastructure and rake in trillions in profits. Carbon capture isn't a serious climate solution. As you can imagine, the folks in Big Oil love it. Vicki Hollub, the CEO of Occidental Petroleum (which just received hundreds of millions from the Department of Energy for carbon capture projects), has said that "direct capture technology is going to be the technology that helps to preserve our industry over time.

This gives our industry a license to continue to operate for the 60, 70, 80 years that I think it's going to be very much needed." Mission accomplished. Carbon capture is being used to distract the world from rapidly phasing out fossil fuels, all on the taxpayer's dime.

It's troubling how many billions of tax dollars have already been wasted on carbon capture boondoggles and Big Oil giveaways. The U.S. Department of Energy has already poured tens of billions into poorly conceived and managed "clean coal" and CCS projects. They have almost entirely failed, earning the condemnation of the Government Accountability Office. And, unbelievably, the U.S. 45Q tax credit for carbon capture projects pays $60 a tonne for carbon used in enhanced oil recovery—which delays the retirement of the fossil fuel industry.

Carbon removal technology could have a role in the fight against climate change, but we would have to use it in a much more targeted way. Hard-to-control industrial sources like cement, steel and fertilizers might be good candidates for specialized CCS projects that can theoretically remove some of these concentrated emissions. This of course is only if researchers, investors and project managers can tackle the technology's technical and financial limitations. Many scientists who are currently critical of carbon capture would support such use.

Bottom line, as we head into COP 28, we need to see fundamental shifts in how carbon capture technology is governed, funded and used in the world. We should forbid any connections between taxpayer-supported carbon capture projects and fossil fuel companies. In the U.S., we should immediately suspend 45Q tax breaks for enhanced oil recovery, which simply subsidize Big Oil's bottom line and increase emissions at taxpayers' expense. All Department of Energy funding for carbon capture projects that benefit fossil fuel interests should also be immediately redirected to more effective climate solutions. And the Government Accountability Office and Congress should continue to investigate how billions of taxpayer dollars ended up subsidizing Big Oil greenwashing—and systems that undermine effective climate action—in the first place. In the end, the global community must never again fall for schemes like this that cost taxpayers billions and remove minimal carbon at enormous cost, while handing Big Oil a PR bonanza.

This is an opinion and analysis article, and the views expressed by the author or authors are not necessarily those of Scientific American.

About the Author

Jonathan Foley is the executive director of Project Drawdown, a nonprofit organization focused on climate solutions. His writing has been featured on the TED stage and in National Geographic, Science, Nature *and numerous other publications. These views are his own.*

Section 2: Biotech Engineering

Millions of Mosquitoes Will Rain Down on Hawaii to Save an Iconic Bird

By Sarah Wild

M illions of mosquitoes dropped from helicopters could be the greatest hope for Hawaii's iconic honeycreepers. At least four species of the brightly colored birds could go extinct in 2024 if no action is taken to save them. "We're seriously in a race against time at the moment," says Hanna Mounce, program manager of the Maui Forest Bird Recovery Project.

These small birds evolved on the islands over the course of millions of years and are uniquely adapted to their niche habitat, where they are crucial pollinators for many of Hawaii's flora. For the people of Hawaii, the honeycreepers are also woven into the cultural fabric, featuring prominently in many legends and providing feathers for traditional garments. More than 50 species of honeycreepers once flitted across the archipelago, but because of introduced predators, habitat destruction and disease, that number has dwindled to only 17. Invasive *Culex quinquefasciatus* mosquitoes—possibly introduced via water barrels on European ships in the early 19th century—pose a particular threat because they spread the deadly avian malaria parasite.

The honeycreepers that still survive today live high in the mountains, where it is too cool for mosquitoes. Rising temperatures are widening the mosquitoes' habitat, however, and every year they move higher up the mountain slopes—and kill birds as they go. Four species of honeycreeper—the 'Akeke'e (*Loxops caeruleirostris*) and the 'Akikiki (*Oreomsytis bairdi*) on the Hawaiian island of Kauai and the Kiwikiu (*Pseudonestor xanthophrys*) and 'Ākohekohe (*Palmeria dolei*) on Maui—are in particularly dire straits. "We have one more warm year, and we're not going to have any birds left," Mounce says.

Birds, Not Mosquitoes, a consortium of more than a dozen state, federal, industry and conservation partners, including the

Maui Forest Bird Recovery Project, is pinning the birds' immediate future on the so-called incompatible insect technique (IIT). To date, this mosquito-control method has only been used for mosquito-borne diseases that affect humans, Mounce says. On two islands in China, for example, the technique cut dengue-carrying mosquito populations by 90 percent.

IIT works like this: *C. quinquefasciatus* mosquitoes, as well as many other arthropods, naturally contain *Wolbachia* bacteria in their gut. In order to produce offspring together, mating mosquitoes must be infected with the same strain of the bacteria. Birds, Not Mosquitoes' plan involves releasing male mosquitoes bred by Verily Life Sciences—the life sciences research arm of Alphabet, which also owns Google. These mosquitos will host a different *Wolbachia* strain than those on Maui. The idea is that the existing female mosquitoes will mate with the male newcomers, but because of their incompatible *Wolbachia* bacteria, they will not produce viable offspring. If all goes according to plan, the overall mosquito population will plummet.

Birds, Not Mosquitoes initially ran trial studies by releasing 5,000 to 30,000 IIT mosquitoes at a time to study their dispersal and longevity in the wild. The team found that although the introduced mosquitoes lived longer than local ones, they did not move far from the release site. This means that future mosquito releases will need to be spaced closer together. For the next phase beginning in November, the consortium will drop 250,000 treated mosquitoes twice a week over about 3,000 acres in east Maui for a year. They will be contained in mango-sized biodegradable capsules that can each hold about 1,000 mosquitoes.

Success, however, hinges not only on reducing mosquito population numbers but also on ensuring that the new *Wolbachia* strain does not establish itself in the local mosquito population. If the local mosquitoes become infected primarily with the new *Wolbachia*, then they will be able to produce offspring with the introduced mosquitoes; that would defeat the goal of the technique and project. To prevent that outcome, the team will set egg traps to check for the new *Wolbachia* strain. If it is found, the project will stop releases "until there is none of that [strain of] *Wolbachia* detected in the landscape before we're able to start again," Mounce says.

Only female mosquitoes bite, and the project is not releasing any females. If the intervention works, the number of female mosquitoes in the release area will plummet, and the next step will be a landscape-wide release of these doctored mosquitoes. "If there are no female mosquitoes in those areas, then they can't bite the birds, and there can't be any malaria transmission," Mounce says. Mosquitoes are not endemic to the islands and woven into native ecosystems in the same way that, for example, honeycreepers are. Consequently, scientists do not expect their removal to harm the environment.

This approach is not a full solution to the birds' plight. Rather "it's a Band-Aid to buy time," says M. Renee Bellinger, a research geneticist at the U.S. Geological Survey, which is one of the consortium's partners. "We recognize that it's not a permanent solution. But it is the solution that is available at the moment and has a regulatory pathway that is defined so that we can get the tool on the landscape." Other concurrent interventions in the U.S. Department of the Interior's Strategy for Preventing the Extinction of Hawaiian Forest Birds include establishing captive care programs, relocating honeycreepers who belong to the most at-risk species, developing gene drive technology to curb mosquitoes' ability to transmit the malaria parasite and increasing birds' malaria resistance.

The IIT plan has a lot of potential, especially in settings such as Hawaii's forests, where insecticide use would be problematic, says Rosemary Lees, a principal research associate at the Liverpool School of Tropical Medicine in England, who is not involved with the project in Hawaii. "As with all new techniques, it will be critical to monitor the effects of the releases, to collect the operational data critical to evaluate impact and maximize cost-effectiveness and coverage," she says.

If the IIT intervention fails, it may be necessary to move the honeycreepers out of mosquito-infested areas. Sam 'Ohu Gon III, a senior scientist and a cultural adviser at the Nature Conservancy, says other islands with higher elevation could provide a refuge to some birds. "Those birds are doomed unless they can be pulled out of that habitat," he says.

But Gon remains optimistic that the IIT will work, at least as a stopgap. "I'm very hopeful," he says, "that it can stave off the fact that some of these birds might be extinct in one or two years if we do nothing."

About the Author

Sarah Wild is a freelance science journalist based in Canterbury in the United Kingdom.

Tiny 'Rover' Explores Cells without Harming Them

By Andrew Chapman

When Deblina Sarkar wanted to name her lab's new creation the "Cell Rover," her students were hesitant. "They were like, 'it seems too cool for a scientific technology,'" she says. But Sarkar, a nanotechnologist at the Massachusetts Institute of Technology, wanted the tiny device's name to evoke exploration of unknown worlds. This rover, however, will roam the inside of a living cell rather than the surface of a planet.

Recent engineering advances have enabled scientists to shrink electronics down to the cellular scale—with hopes of potentially using them to explore and manipulate the innards of individual cells. But such a rover would need to receive instructions and transmit information—and communicating with devices this small can be extremely difficult. "Miniaturizing an antenna to fit inside the cell is a key challenge," Sarkar says. The problem involves the electromagnetic waves that are used with most conventional antennas, like those in cell phones, to transmit and receive data. Antennas operate best at their so-called "resonant frequencies," which occur at wavelengths roughly equal to the antenna's actual length. Because of the mathematical relationship between a wave's speed, frequency and wavelength, waves with shorter wavelengths have higher frequencies. Unfortunately, subcellular antennas have to be so tiny that they require frequencies in the microwave range. And like the beams in a kitchen microwave, these signals "just fry up the cells," Sarkar says. But she and her colleagues think they have a solution. In a *Nature Communications* paper, they describe a new antenna design that can operate safely inside cells by resonating with acoustic rather than electromagnetic waves. A functioning antenna could help scientists power, and communicate with, tiny roving sensors within the cell, helping them better understand these building blocks and perhaps leading to new medical treatments.

Sarkar and her team machined their experimental antenna from a "magnetostrictive" material—one that changes shape when exposed to a magnetic field. The researchers chose a widely available alloy of iron, nickel, boron and molybdenum, a combination already used in other kinds of sensors. When an alternating-current magnetic field is applied to this magnetostrictive antenna, the north and south poles of its molecules align themselves with the changing magnetic field, flipping back and forth, which stretches the material. This motion makes the antenna vibrate like a tiny tuning fork. Like any magnetic material, the antenna produces its own magnetic field in response to the external one, but because it is vibrating, its motion alters its new magnetic field in ways that a receiver can detect. This allows for two-way communication.

The key difference between a conventional antenna and the Cell Rover is the translation of electromagnetic waves into acoustic waves. "Their antenna resonates not based on the wavelength of light, but on the wavelength of sound," explains Jacob Robinson, a Rice University neuroengineer who was not involved in the study. Like larger traditional antennas, the Cell Rover hits its resonant frequency when waves have a wavelength equal to its length—but the waves that stimulate this frequency are sound waves, which travel much more slowly than electromagnetic waves. Because the relationship between a wave's wavelength and frequency also depends on its speed, sound waves and electromagnetic waves with the same wavelength will have different frequencies. In other words, the external magnetic field can signal the Cell Rover using waves with frequencies outside the harmful microwave range. "It's a clever approach," Robinson says.

The researchers first tested the Cell Rover in air and water, and they found that the antenna's frequency of operation was 10,000 times smaller than that of an equivalent electromagnetic antenna—low enough to avoid killing live cells. Next the team tested the device within a living system: the egg cell of the African clawed frog, a model organism. Since the Cell Rover was made from a magnetic material, the researchers could use a magnet to pull it into each test cell. After these insertions, the egg cells looked healthy under a microscope and had not sprung any leaks. While inside the egg cell, the Cell Rover was able to receive an electromagnetic transmission and send a responding signal outward, up to a distance of one centimeter. The researchers also added multiple different-sized Cell Rovers to a single cell, and found they could distinguish the transmission signals of individual rovers.

Despite the progress in shrinking the Cell Rover, the prototypes themselves were still relatively large. At just over 400 micrometers (0.4 millimeters) long, they were too sizeable to fit inside many cell types. So the scientists computationally simulated the operation of an antenna about 20 times smaller than the ones they tested. They found these hypothetical rovers could retain a similar communication range—but they have yet to build them. Robinson says the range will also have to be increased to enable such devices to work in living organisms. "I think more work needs to be done to add functionality," Robinson adds. "They are not yet doing anything biologically relevant."

So far the scientists have only showed that the Cell Rover can work in principle, using it to send empty signals; this type of transmission can be thought of as being a little like static on a TV. Next they will try to determine what kind of "shows" they can watch by outfitting the rover with tiny instruments that could collect and convey information about the rover's surroundings. For instance, they might add a simple polymer coating that would bind to nearby ions or proteins. When these substances stick to the polymer they would change the Cell Rover's mass, and this in turn would alter the acoustic vibrations it produces. By measuring these changes, researchers could assess a cell's protein or ion levels.

A Cell Rover might also be adapted for more complex applications. It might be possible to someday use such devices to destroy cancer cells, to electrically alter signaling pathways in order to influence cell division or differentiation, or even to serve as a power source for other miniature devices. "We can not only do intracellular sensing and modulate the intracellular activities, but we can power nanoelectronic circuits," Sarkar says. Such miniscule electronics could also steer the Cell Rover on an exploratory journey, like its much-larger namesakes: they would allow it to analyze sensor data and modify the cellular environment without a scientist's input. "It will someday be able to make autonomous decisions," Sarkar says. "The opportunities are just limitless."

About the Author

Andrew Chapman is a Truckee, Calif.–based freelance science writer who covers life sciences and the environment.

Tiny, Tumbling Origami Robots Could Help with Targeted Drug Delivery

By Fionna M. D. Samuels

A new kind of hollow, pea-sized robot can roll, flip and jump to navigate its surroundings. It can transition from dry surfaces to pools of liquid with ease, making it fully amphibious. Its ability to use different types of motion in multiple environments—while carrying a cargo—sets it apart from other wee machines, most of which can only move in a single way. The new bot's versatility also makes it uniquely adept at working its way through, over and around obstacles. One day its small size and multifunctionality might let it navigate the complex environment of a human body and deliver a targeted payload of medicine to a patient in need.

The robot's ability to overcome physical obstacles stems from a unique design: creased in an origami arrangement called a Kresling pattern and topped with a magnet. The Kresling pattern looks like a series of stacked right triangles wrapping around the robot's belly, making it resemble a ridged and slightly squashed cylinder. The ridges also give it a propellerlike shape that helps it move through liquid. "What we really wanted to see is whether we could integrate the geometric features with the foldability of the origami design to achieve effective navigation of the [robot] and also use its foldability mechanism for drug delivery," says Renee Zhao, an assistant professor of mechanical engineering at Stanford University. She and her colleagues describe the robot in a paper published in 2022 in *Nature Communications*.

A small hole at one end offers access to the robot's hollow center, which can hold a small payload: an object or some liquid. A magnet at the other end allows the machine to be controlled wirelessly—all the operator needs is their own magnet. The kind of magnetic field the researchers used is similar to the type generated by a magnetic resonance imaging (MRI) machine, Zhao explains.

"I think one strategy would be developing this robot so that it's compatible with the MRI system," she says, in order to control it while a patient is in the imaging machine. Developing a new kind of device that could generate and manipulate the correct kind of magnetic field is also an option, Zhao adds, but it would need to incorporate medical imaging like an MRI machine does to track the robot's location within the body.

Some versions of the new robot have a second magnet on the opposite side of its soft, cylindrical structure. This makes the bot pumpable. An operator controlling the magnetic field generates a small amount of rotational force between the magnets, which squeezes the robot's thin plastic body. Doing this repeatedly can pump liquid from the robot's belly to its surroundings.

The device can do more than deliver liquid payloads. Its propellerlike shape means an operator can make it spin by applying a rotating magnetic field—and thereby push it through liquids. This spinning also generates enough suction to pull objects into the robot's hollow belly. And as it swims, the spinning motion holds the sucked-up payload inside. When the robot reaches its destination, the operator can stop the spinning, and the bot will dump out whatever it has picked up. This allows delivery of small solid payloads to targeted locations.

In theory, this process could carry liquid or solid medications directly to specific locations in a body—possibly in the digestive tract, for example. The robot was designed with materials that are soft enough to avoid tissue damage, Zhao says. Even the magnet is squishy, she points out. The team made it by embedding tiny glass beads and metal nanoparticles in pliable plastic. The researchers demonstrated that the robot can maneuver through the dry environment of an empty pig's stomach, as well as one filled with liquid. They controlled the robot's general trajectory, but there was no need to tell it how to maneuver around small obstacles: the magnetic field told it to move in a certain direction, and it rolled, tumbled or performed whatever other movement it took to take that path. If the robot encountered a larger obstacle, its operator could briefly increase the magnetic field's strength to make the bot jump. If it ran into a deep pool of liquid, the operator could change the magnetic field so the device would swim.

This multifunctionality in such a simply designed robot surprised Siyi Xu, a postdoctoral robotics engineer at the Harvard Microrobotics Laboratory, who was not involved in the new study. "It is very interesting to see them achieve many of these abilities into one integrated [design]," she says. Xu adds that many similar small robots only specialize in one kind of motion, be it walking, crawling, swimming or flying.

The new, more adept origami design could be like a blueprint for future tiny robots, Zhao says. That could open up more applications. "These functionalities are not limited to a specific disease or a specific application," she says. She and her lab are now considering how these robots might be made even smaller and able to travel in the bloodstream. Slightly larger bots could carry tiny cameras or forceps, which would be useful for minimally invasive medical procedures. Zhao plans to continue exploring similar devices, adding even more capabilities to these microrobots while maintaining their simplicity of design.

About the Author

Fionna M. D. Samuels was a 2022 AAAS Mass Media Fellow at Scientific American. She's pursuing a Ph.D. in chemistry at Colorado State University. Follow her on X (formerly Twitter) @Fairy__Hedgehog.

This Sticker Looks Inside the Body

By Sophie Bushwick

U ltrasound scanners, which image the inside of the human body, are a life-saving medical tool. Now researchers have shrunk the handheld ultrasound probe—which typically requires a highly trained technician to move over the skin—down to a flat chip that is the size of a postage stamp and sticks to the skin with a special bioadhesive. The new device can record high-resolution videos for two days at a stretch, capturing blood vessels and hearts laboring during exercise or stomachs expanding and shrinking as test subjects gulp juice and then digest it.

"The beauty of this is, suddenly, you can adhere this ultrasound probe, this thin ultrasound speaker, to the body over 48 hours," says Xuanhe Zhao, a mechanical engineer at the Massachusetts Institute of Technology and co-author of a paper describing the new device, which was published in *Science* on Thursday. By recording still pictures and videos of internal organs during this time, a wearable imaging device could be used to diagnose heart attacks and malignant tumors, test the effectiveness of medications and assess general heart, lung or muscle health. "This can potentially change the paradigm of medical imaging by empowering long-term continuous imaging," Zhao adds, "and it can change the paradigm of the field of wearable devices."

Traditional ultrasounds are great at peering beneath the skin without causing damage to the body, but access to such scans is limited. "The conventional handheld ultrasound requires well-trained technicians to put the probe properly on the skin and apply some liquid gel between the probe and skin," says Nanshu Lu, a mechanical engineer at the University of Texas at Austin, who was not involved in the new research but co-wrote an accompanying analysis in *Science*. "And as you can imagine, it's quite tedious and very short-term, very constrained." Because they require an experienced human operator, Lu explains, these scans are expensive, and they cannot be used in tests where the subject is exercising or putting their body under stress from heat or extreme environments. "Conventional ultrasounds have a lot of limitations," she says. "If we can make ultrasound sensors wearable and mobile and accessible, it will open a lot of new possibilities."

Thanks to their potential versatility, other researchers have attempted to make stick-on ultrasound patches. But in order to adhere to soft, stretchy skin, earlier devices were designed to be stretchable themselves. This form factor weakened image quality because it could not accommodate as many transducers—units that, in this case, transform electrical power into sound waves with frequencies too high for human ears to detect. An ultrasound probe sends these waves through a layer of gooey gel into the human body, where they bounce off organs and other internal structures and then return to the transducer array. This converts the mechanical waves back to electrical signals and sends them to a computer for translation into images.

The more transducers, the better the image quality. "It's very similar to a camera," explains Philip Tan, an electrical engineer and a graduate student at Lu's lab at U.T. Austin, who was also not involved with the new study but co-wrote the analysis piece. A stretchy stick-on ultrasound probe, which must be able to flex every time the skin moves, cannot pack as many transducers into the array—and when the wearer moves, the configuration of transducers shifts and makes it difficult to capture stable images.

Instead of making the device itself stretchy, Zhao and his team attached a rigid probe, just three millimeters thick, to a flexible layer of adhesive. This adhesive replaces the gooey liquid placed between a traditional ultrasound wand and the skin, and it is a hybrid of a water-rich polymer called a hydrogel and a rubberlike material called an elastomer. "It is a piece of solid hydrogel containing over 90 percent water, but it is in a solid state like Jell-O," Zhao says. "We cover the surface of this Jell-O with this very thin membrane of elastomer so that the water inside the Jell-O will not evaporate out." This bioadhesive not only stuck the probe firmly to the skin for 48 hours, but it also provided a cushioning layer that protected the rigid electronics from the flexing of skin and muscles.

To image different body systems, Zhao's team tested versions of the probe that produce waves at different frequencies and thus penetrate the body to different depths. For instance, a high frequency such as 10 megahertz might make it to a couple of centimeters beneath the skin. The researchers used this frequency to capture the action of blood vessels and muscles as test subjects shifted from sitting to standing or exercised vigorously. A lower frequency of three megahertz goes deeper, more like six centimeters, to capture internal organs. Using this frequency, the researchers imaged the four chambers of a subject's heart, and recorded the stomach of another emptying out as their system processed a couple of cups of juice. The researchers also compared the images gathered with their rigid ultrasound probe with those captured by a stretchable ultrasound device, Zhao says. "You can see the resolution of ours is almost one order of magnitude [10 times] higher than the stretchable ultrasound," he adds.

An imaging device that maintains a continuous watch over specific parts of the body could be used to monitor and diagnose a variety of ailments. Doctors could keep a close eye on the growth of a tumor over time. Someone at high risk of hypertension might wear an ultrasound patch to measure their high blood pressure, alerting them when the pressure spikes or tracking whether a medication is helping. A COVID patient could stay home, knowing that an imaging device would alert them if their illness caused a lung infection severe enough to require hospitalization. Perhaps the most important application could be in the detection and diagnosis of heart attacks. "Cardiovascular disease is ... the leading cause of death in the whole world, also in the U.S.," Zhao says. Heart health is on the radar of other wearable device developers. For instance, smart watches such as the Apple Watch are capable of tracking the electrical signals that indicate heart activity with a so-called electrocardiogram (ECG or EKG). This can be used to diagnose heart attacks—at least in some cases. "There are already studies showing that EKG can only diagnose around 20 percent of heart attacks. The majority of heart attacks actually require imaging modalities, such as ultrasound imaging, to diagnose," Zhao says. Continuous imaging of a patient's heart could capture their symptoms and provide an early diagnosis.

"The big selling point of this new device is that it opens new types of medical diagnosis that can't be done in a static setting," Tan says. To assess heart health, for instance, it's helpful to measure the organ's activity while exercising—but it's hard to hold an ultrasound wand against a running subject's goo-covered chest. "With a wearable ultrasound patch, where you wouldn't have to hold the transducer on the person, they were actually able to show that you're able to get very high-quality images of the heart even during motion," Tan adds.

The bioadhesive device is not ready for action yet, however. For one thing, it still has to be physically plugged into a computer that can collect and analyze the data the probe produces. "We connect this probe through a wire to a data acquisition system," Zhao says. "But my group is working very hard to miniaturize and integrate everything into our wireless device." He ultimately plans to upgrade the patch with a miniaturized power source and a wireless data-transmission system. This is a feasible goal, Lu and Tan agree, thanks to shrinking electronic components and fabrication methods that allow these features to be combined into an "ultrasound on a chip." Lu suggests that if the field can attract federal and private investments, such a device could be feasible within five years, although it would still have to earn approval from federal regulators.

Ultimately, ultrasound stickers could join the ranks of wearables that monitor human health, including existing devices that gather information about heart rate, sleep quality and even stress. "Our human body is radiating a lot of a highly personal, highly continuous, distributed and multimodal data about our health, our emotion, our attention, our readiness, and so on. So we're full of data," Lu says. "The question is how to get them reliably and continuously."

About the Author

Sophie Bushwick is tech editor at Scientific American. *She runs the daily technology news coverage for the website, writes about everything from artificial intelligence to jumping robots for both digital and print publication, records YouTube and TikTok videos and hosts the podcast* Tech, Quickly. *Bushwick also makes frequent appearances on radio shows such as* Science Friday *and television networks, including* CBS, MSNBC *and National Geographic. She has more than a decade of experience as a science journalist based in New York City and previously worked at outlets such as* Popular Science, Discover *and* Gizmodo. *Follow Bushwick on X (formerly Twitter) @sophiebushwick.*

Why Is It So Hard to Make Vegan Fish?

By Joanna Thompson

When I went vegetarian a decade ago, I found it pretty painless to pass on most animal-based dishes. Burgers? Plant-based patties were abundant and, for the most part, delicious. Poultry? Easy: vegan chicken nuggets tasted just like the real deal. Pork? I'd never been a huge fan in the first place. My one weakness was sushi. No matter where I looked, I just couldn't find a satisfying veggie alternative to my favorite form of seafood.

It's only now, 10 years later, that new food science innovations could finally make the vegan, whole-cut fish of my dreams a reality. This year several alternative protein companies are launching or already offering their first crop of plant-based filets, promising to replicate the taste and texture of real fish. But why is it so hard to make a good piece of vegan salmon in the first place?

It turns out that flavor is the easy part. The rather specific taste common to fresh fish comes mostly from a combination of molecules that scientists already know how to replicate in a lab: long-chain fatty acids, such as omega-3s and omega-6s, which give fish their oily quality and taste, and volatile carbonyls, which lend a lighter, almost melonlike flavor. The real challenge of vegan fish is nailing the mouthfeel. "When the texture is enjoyable, you can take the dish in many directions," says Guy Vaknin, a chef who heads four vegan restaurants in New York City, including Beyond Sushi. "It's a great canvas."

"Fish has a very special texture," says Atze Jan van der Goot, a food process engineer at Wageningen University & Research in the Netherlands. Most cuts of fish actually contain several layers of short-fiber muscle, which are held together with thin bands of connective tissue and fat. Within each layer, bundles of microscopic muscle fibers are arranged like the teeth of a comb, all pointing in the same direction. It's this structure that gives cooked fish its unique flaky quality.

But most processes for making meat substitutes aren't designed to mimic muscle fiber. Instead they aim for a far simpler consistency: that of ground meat, which can be pressed into burger patty, sausage or nugget form. "I think a lot of meat is consumed via nugget-type products," van der Goot says, "especially in the U.S."

The food-processing technique that best achieves nugget texture in vegetarian meat substitutes is called extrusion. It involves grinding raw food material, such as grains, vegetable proteins and various additives, into fine particles and then forcing the resulting "dough" through a tube under high pressure. As it squeezes through this opening, the food slurry is cooked simultaneously by added steam and the heat of its own friction.

Like the *Star Trek* "replicator," extruders can squirt out an astronomical range of prepackaged edibles—everything from Cheerios to cheese puffs to chewing gum relies on this process. The catch is that such products all have a similar texture, and they can't be extruded raw. The process generates so much heat that it denatures, or unravels, most of the available protein molecules in the extruded material, rendering it somewhat shapeless. This is perfectly fine if people want to purchase a vegan crab cake. But it presents a challenge if they're shopping for a raw fish substitute in order to re-create the experience of, say, biting into uncooked salmon crudo or searing a juicy tuna steak.

Luckily, food scientists are now finding creative new ways to re-create fish's intricate sheets of parallel muscle fiber. One such technique is called directional freezing. This process capitalizes on the fact that ice tends to form in a certain direction—starting from the coldest point and moving outward. It also tends to adhere to itself, freezing in pure crystals of H_2O. Some food researchers have applied directional freezing to blocks of gel made from edible algae. As the gel freezes, the water inside it solidifies into needlelike ice structures, creating a matrix of thousands of tiny tubes. This perforated gel makes a great scaffolding for uncooked faux fish.

That's the strategy that New School Foods, a Canadian alternative meat start-up, is using to craft its plant-based raw salmon and tuna filets. "It's basically like a directional sponge," says Auke de Vries, New School Foods' lead food materials scientist. Adjusting the size of the gel matrix or tweaking its freezing temperature can yield differently sized or shaped channels, "which is important because that's the main driver of texture," de Vries says.

Once the scaffolding is in place, the food science researchers can fill the channels by injecting them with whatever mixture of protein, fat and flavor they want. The options include 100 percent plant-based proteins, such as soy, pea or gluten, and—potentially—actual animal cells cultured in the lab. They can also add volatile flavor compounds that might otherwise break down in a precooked product. "We're not married to any one ingredient," says New School Foods founder Chris Bryson.

But there's more than one way to skin a vegan catfish. Another method gaining traction in the alternative seafood world is 3-D printing. Revo Foods, a plant-based seafood manufacturer in Vienna, uses 3-D food printers to build smoked salmon filets from the ground up with carefully constructed layers of pea protein, algal extracts and omega-3 fatty acids.

If all of these techniques sound elaborate, it's because they are. But the technology to make vegan meat and seafood is getting cheaper by the day, and its proponents believe the environmental benefits far outweigh the production hassle. "The impact that overfishing and harmful fishing practices have on vulnerable ocean ecosystems is very serious," says Birgit Dekkers, a food scientist and co-founder of the Dutch plant-based meat company Rival Foods.

According to the Food and Agriculture Organization of the United Nations, overfishing and habitat destruction have depleted more than one third of global fish stocks. Not only does this wreak havoc on aquatic ecosystems, it can even contribute to global climate change by reducing the number of species available to store carbon. "The overall carbon footprint of ocean trawling is equivalent to the carbon footprint of the entire aviation industry," Bryson says.

Persuading more people to switch to sustainable plant-based seafood isn't going to fix climate change. But it could be a step toward ensuring that there are always plenty of fish in the sea.

About the Author

Joanna Thompson is an insect enthusiast and former Scientific American *intern. She is based in New York City. Follow Thompson on X (formerly Twitter) @jojofoshosho0.*

Synthetic Enamel Could Make Teeth Stronger and Smarter

By Joanna Thompson

E namel, the tough outer covering of a tooth, is the hardest substance in the human body. It is also notoriously difficult to replicate artificially. Throughout history, dentists have repaired damaged and decayed teeth with everything from beeswax to mercury composites to modern ceramic- or resin-based materials. But they might soon have a synthetic option that is much closer to the real thing.

A team of chemical and structural engineers has invented a new material that mimics enamel's fundamental properties: It is strong and—very importantly—also slightly elastic. This versatile substance could potentially be used to reinforce fractured bones, craft better pacemakers and, beyond serving as a replacement for dental enamel, take fillings to the next level by creating "smart teeth." A study on this work was published in 2022 in *Science*.

Natural enamel has the difficult job of protecting teeth, which are constantly being strained by oral bacteria, acidic foods, chewing and even speaking. Over time, the wear and tear adds up. "You carry the same set of teeth for 60 years, or maybe even more," says Nicholas Kotov, a chemical engineer at the University of Michigan and co-author of the study. "So it's an enormous chemical and mechanical stress." And unlike bone, enamel cannot be regenerated by the human body.

Enamel's crucial combination of toughness and flexibility is tricky to reproduce. "Soft materials are normally easier to manufacture," Kotov explains. The secret to enamel's uniquely balanced properties lies in its structure. It is composed of millions of closely packed rods of calcium phosphate, which are only visible through an electron microscope.

"Imagine a pack of pencils when you hold them together," says Janet Moradian-Oldak, a biochemist at the University of Southern California who was not involved in the research. This arrangement allows the rods to compress slightly under pressure, rather than shattering, while also keeping the overall structure extremely strong. The artificial enamel mimics this configuration, bundling calcium phosphate rods together with flexible polymer chains.

The researchers fashioned their new material into a tooth shape, then tested whether it would crack under intense heat and pressure. "It's actually very elegant the way that these authors use engineering and harsh laboratory conditions to mimic what cells and nature do," Moradian-Oldak says. Ultimately, the team found the artificial enamel could withstand more force than the natural kind.

The material may not be a perfect tooth analogue, however. "I don't see much answered in the paper to mimic the 3-D structure of human enamel," says Thomas Diekwisch, a craniofacial researcher at Texas A&M University, who was not involved in the new study. But, he notes, that doesn't mean it won't be useful. "At least for functional biomimicry, you don't have to exactly reproduce what nature does."

Outside of its obvious potential in dentistry, Kotov envisions the material being used to build better and longer-lasting pacemakers for people with heart conditions, or to reinforce crumbling bone in those with severe osteoporosis. He says the material could even be modified to create a "smart tooth," a prosthetic chomper containing sensors that could sync to a smartphone. Such a device could monitor a person's breath and mouth bacteria for anomalies, which would allow doctors to catch conditions such as diabetes before a patient is aware of them.

But before it can debut in the dentist's office, the material has to be affordable, mass producible, and clinically tested for safety and efficacy. "I'm impressed with the approach that they use," Moradian-Oldak says. "The question is, how practical is it?"

Kotov says his team used strictly biocompatible compounds in the fabrication process, which means the artificial enamel should theoretically be safe for humans. He hopes to see it used in the next few years, but he isn't making any projections. Paraphrasing a quote that's been attributed to figures including Niels Bohr and Yogi Berra, Kotov says, "It's very difficult to predict anything—especially the future."

About the Author

Joanna Thompson is an insect enthusiast and former Scientific American intern. She is based in New York City. Follow Thompson on X (formerly Twitter) @jojofoshosho0.

Soft Robot Hand Is First to Be Fully 3-D-Printed in a Single Step

By Sophie Bushwick

A soft robotic hand has finally achieved a historic accomplishment: beating the first level of Super Mario Bros. Although quickly pressing and releasing the buttons and directional pad on a Nintendo Entertainment System controller is a fun test of this three-fingered machine's performance, the real breakthrough is not what it does— but how it was created.

The Mario-playing hand, as well as two turtlelike "soft robots" described in the same recent *Science Advances* paper, were each 3-D-printed in a single process that only took three to eight hours. "Every one of those robots in this paper was 100 percent no-assembly-required-printed," says co-author Ryan Sochol, an assistant professor of mechanical engineering at the University of Maryland.

One-step production would make it easier for researchers to develop increasingly complex soft robots. These bots' squishy makeup lets them interact with delicate materials—such as tissues in a human body—without the kind of damage more rigid machines might cause. This makes them good candidates for tasks such as performing surgery or search and rescue and even sorting fruit or other easily damaged items. But so far most such bots still include at least some rigid components. It was not until 2016 that researchers created one entirely from flexible materials. To make that octopuslike soft robot work, its creators had to ditch rigid electronic circuits for a microfluidic one. In such circuits, water or air moves through microchannels; its flow is modified by fluid-based analogues to electronic components such as transistors and diodes.

In the study, the researchers stepped up the development of this technology. "They introduced much more complicated microfluidic circuits," says Harvard University engineering professor Jennifer Lewis, who co-authored the 2016 paper but was not involved in the University of Maryland's project. In the Mario-playing hand, for example, the circuit allowed a single source of fluid to send different signals, telling each finger to move independently by simply varying the input pressure.

Printing It Up

But in making soft robots more sophisticated, fluidic circuits also render the machines harder to manufacture and assemble. That is why Sochol is so excited about printing them in one step. "Never once has it been done all in a single run," he says, "to have an entire soft robot with all of the integrated fluidic circuitry and the body features and the soft actuators [moving parts] all printed."

He and his colleagues used a PolyJet 3-D printer, a type that sets down a liquid layer, exposes it to a light that solidifies it and then adds the next layer. The model they employed, manufactured by a company called Stratasys, could produce three types of material: a soft rubberlike substance, a more rigid plasticlike one and a water-soluble "sacrificial material" that acts as scaffolding during printing but must be removed from the final product afterward.

Such high-tech printers can retail for tens of thousands of dollars—but Sochol's team did not need to buy one. "We use a service on campus to do this," he says. "So we sent our files to them, they printed it, and then we picked it up." Sochol estimates that anyone else wanting to print one of these designs—which his team shared as open-access software on the development site GitHub—could use a similar 3-D-printing service for about $100 or less.

Sochol contends this process is faster, cheaper and easier than fabricating a microfluidic circuit in a clean room, creating a robot separately and then combining them later. Lewis does not entirely agree. "There's an elegance to it. I'm not sure it's faster, cheaper, necessarily," she says. "But there is cumbersome nature to having to create the circuit by one method and then insert it, like we did, into a molded and 3-D-printed robot. And I would say that the method that [Sochol and his colleagues] chose ... has many advantages in terms of being able to print multiple materials of different stiffness." Lewis also points out that the new soft bot is not ready to go immediately after printing. "One cumbersome part of their method is that you have to remove all the sacrificial material," she says. "And when it's on the outside of the body, just as support, that's fine. But it's also present in all of those internal channels."

It's-a Me, Mario!

After cleaning up their printed robots, Sochol's team had to design a performance test. Earlier studies have programmed robotic fingers to play a tune on a piano, for example, but Sochol's team thought that task was too easy. "With that, we could set the tempo arbitrarily, he says. "If the robot misses a note or something like that, there's no meaningful penalties." Video games seemed a little more uncompromising. "If you make a mistake, if we don't press the button at the right time or we don't [release] the button at the right time, you can run into an enemy, you can fall down a pit, and it's an immediate game over," Sochol says.

The researchers placed their three-fingered robotic hand on a Nintendo controller, with each finger laid on a different button or the directional pad. By feeding fluid through a control line at different pressures, they could make each finger respond. "For a low pressure, the circuit is able to respond to that and press only the button that causes Mario to move forward," Sochol explains. "And then for a medium pressure, a second finger begins to press a button, and now Mario can run. And then if it's a high pressure, then all three fingers will be pressing their respective buttons, and Mario will jump."

The team wrote a computer program that would change the pressure automatically, causing the fingers to move in a set pattern. Because people have been playing Super Mario Bros. for decades, the team knew exactly what sequence of buttons the hand would need to press to win the game's first level. It just had to run through that preprogrammed list with the correct timing—which is harder than it sounds. The challenging part, Sochol says, was "getting it to not just press a button but then stop pressing it and then repress it, because there's a lot of times where Mario has to jump and then jump again very quickly as he's running."

"The Mario part is kind of cute and certainly will be attention-grabbing," Lewis says. "But I think what's really powerful about this paper is the multimaterial 3-D printing, the ability to integrate all of this complex fluidic circuitry in one fab step. There's really a lot to like about what [the researchers have] done."

Winning the video game showed that the fully printed robotic hand could respond swiftly and accurately to a changing input. Any well-known video game could have made this point, but Mario holds a special place in many players' hearts. "We felt like this was the baseline game," Sochol says. "When I was a four- or five-year-old, and we got a Nintendo system, that was the very first thing that I played ever."

About the Author

Sophie Bushwick is tech editor at Scientific American. *She runs the daily technology news coverage for the website, writes about everything from artificial intelligence to jumping robots for both digital and print publication, records YouTube and TikTok videos and hosts the podcast* Tech, Quickly. *Bushwick also makes frequent appearances on radio shows such as* Science Friday *and television networks, including CBS, MSNBC and National Geographic. She has more than a decade of experience as a science journalist based in New York City and previously worked at outlets such as* Popular Science, Discover *and* Gizmodo. *Follow Bushwick on X (formerly Twitter) @sophiebushwick.*

Section 3: AI and Us

Drones Could Spot Crime Scenes from Afar

By Rachel Berkowitz

V olunteers sometimes spend months trudging through remote terrain to search for lost hikers or crime victims. But a new tool could soon pinpoint forensic evidence from the sky instead. By identifying how traces of blood and other human signs reflect light when found on various natural surfaces, the scientists say searchers will be able to quickly scour large areas for clues about missing persons—dead or alive—using images acquired by drones.

Special drone-mounted sensors can record wavelength intensity for the entire electromagnetic spectrum (rather than just the red, green and blue of a typical camera) in each pixel of an image. Geologists routinely use this technology to pinpoint mineral deposits. Mark Krekeler, a mineralogist at Miami University in Ohio, and his colleagues realized that the same approach, supported by the right spectral data library, could potentially detect forensic evidence.

To build their tool, the researchers measured how human-related features, including blood, sweaty clothing and skin tones, reflect different wavelengths of light. Previous studies have examined such reflective "signatures" to identify blood, "but the signature depends on the surface itself and may change over time," Krekeler says. He and his team analyzed thousands of samples, such as bloodstains on different rock types, recording how they changed as the blood dried.

The researchers customized software that mixes the known reflective signatures of various surfaces to reproduce a target of interest. For example, rock and clothing signatures can be combined to seek a hiker lost in the mountains, or a blood signature can be mixed with those of clothing and sand to search for a wounded person in a desert.

The software estimates whether the target exists in any pixel in an image. It can distinguish between an animal and a human in dense forest, search a cityscape for evidence of a specific person in a blue cotton dress, or determine whether soil is stained by blood or diesel fuel, Krekeler says. His team was slated to present its work at the Geological Society of America's meeting of the North-Central Section in April.

Wendy Calvin, a planetary scientist at the University of Nevada, Reno, who was not involved with the study, calls it "an interesting and novel use of spectral data—and the technique looks promising." But she says it could be challenging to use from afar because of how much of a substance would likely be needed to show up in a pixel.

Within months, officials will be able to download and test the tool for themselves. Developing best-practice protocols for search teams could make such technology routine for investigations and forensics, Krekeler says. As drones and sensors become more widespread, he adds, they can transform investigations that are currently costly, labor-intensive or even impossible.

About the Author

Rachel Berkowitz is a freelance science writer and a corresponding editor for Physics Magazine. *She is based in Vancouver, British Columbia, and Eastsound, Wash*

Firefighting Robots Go Autonomous

By Jane Braxton Little

F irefighting, one of the nation's most tradition-bound professions, is poised for an influx of eccentric assistants. They range from contraptions the size of a toy wagon to two-ton beasts that resemble military tanks and can blast out 2,500 gallons of water per minute. Some move on rubber tires, some on steel tracks, and some fly. All are robots.

At a time when more than 3,000 Americans die in fires each year—including an average of 80 firefighters—these high-tech devices can enter burning buildings too hot for human survival. They can penetrate smoke too toxic for human lungs. They are often faster, stronger and more agile than the firefighters they work with. Most of the machines currently in use are remote-controlled, but researchers are now developing "intelligent" firefighting robots that can make decisions autonomously.

Autonomous or not, no one expects machines to completely replace humans on the fire line. Robots are tools, explains Giuseppe Loianno, an assistant professor at New York University—and one valuable thing they can do is reduce risks to human firefighters. With more than 350,000 American homes burning annually, and climate change contributing to 10,000 active daily wildfires worldwide, robots can offer some respite to firefighters entering blazing buildings or traversing steep mountainsides. The main challenge these machines face is institutional reluctance to invest in devices tailored to meet these varying niche needs. "This is not a technological problem. It's more of a socioeconomic problem," says Neil Sahota, an inventor who advises the United Nations on artificial intelligence issues.

Researchers are working to change this. One of the most affordable automatons developed thus far was built by a group of university students using widely available off-the-shelf materials. An unassuming machine resembling a teched-out, canary yellow go-cart, it carries a water tank and a shoebox-size PC; the latter uses information from onboard sensors to move around without crashing into obstacles. A skinny arm protrudes above the chassis and can bend in several places, including an upper "elbow" that twists into angles beyond what a human limb could tolerate. The arm is tipped with a heat-sensing camera, another camera that measures depth and color, and a nozzle. In a recent demonstration this robot pauses in a doorway to get its geospatial bearings, then rolls smoothly into position to assess the room. The tip of the arm rotates, scanning the walls in search of a heat source. When it finds one, it aims the nozzle and opens up, spraying water in a grid pattern precisely over the hotspot. The fire out, the robot pauses in a puddle as if taking a ceremonial bow. It recently won the 2020 Mohamed Bin Zayed International Robotics Challenge.

What makes this working-class cousin to R2-D2 unique is the way its student designers combined hardware components with software intelligence, says Loianno, who coordinated the project. The students demonstrated that an autonomous firefighter can be built for around $40,000 to $50,000—even as little as $10,000—by using less-expensive components, Loianno adds. That's 30 times cheaper than the cost of some firefighting bots currently in use.

This autonomous bot has yet to be tested in a real-world fire, however. Mobility is the big complication, says Sahota, who was not involved in the student collaboration. It is possible to program a robot to manipulate stairwells or even do backflips, Sahota notes. But adapting an autonomous robot for unexpected and uneven terrains remains daunting, he says.

A human-controlled robot called Robotics Systems 3 (RS3), now in use by the Los Angeles City Fire Department, has met some of these real-world mobility challenges and proved useful by dragging hose lines up steep hills and even pulling horses out of mud quagmires, says LAFD Assistant Chief Wade White. The $300,000 RS3, American-made and funded through the fire department's foundation, has also worked with firefighters in buildings with collapsing roofs—"places where we could potentially lose a human life," White says.

At 3,500 pounds with a massive yellow plow nose, tanklike treads and a nozzle that can blast water at 10 times the rate of a conventional fire hose, the RS3 is certainly less vulnerable than its human coworkers—but it still relies on one of them to control it. From a safe distance of 900 feet, operators can view video and temperature information from four cameras that monitor the robot's surroundings. One camera, mounted on the nozzle, shows where the water spray is directed. Another uses thermal imaging to help an operator find any potential victims. Unlike the case with the students' autonomous device, the people running RS3 and other human-operated robots "are processing all this information and making decisions based on ... input" from the devices, White says. That distinguishes RS3 and other human-operated robots from the students' project. "It will never replace firefighters," White says. Instead, it is a tool that allows humans to choose effective strategies without risking their lives.

Faced with steadily worsening wildfires in the American West, the U.S. Forest Service has been dabbling with remote-controlled firefighting technologies since the early 2000s. Its program began in earnest in 2018, driven by four firefighter-carrying helicopter crashes since 2010. "That's 16 fatalities in eight years," says Dirk Giles, manager of the agency's Unmanned Aircraft Systems program. "We needed to deploy technologies to get our employees out of that dead man's curve." After flying observational drones for several years to gather information about fire conditions, the agency added "dragon eggs" to its arsenal. Remote-controlled aircraft drop spheres the size of ping-pong balls, filled with two compounds: potassium permanganate and glycol. They descend through the canopy to the ground, where the chemicals react to start small and deliberate fires. These controlled burns aim to return fire to its natural role in the landscape, where it helps keep forest fuels at more balanced levels. Since the program started, the Forest Service has used dragon eggs to start about 200,000 acres of intentional burns.

In summer 2021, the agency adapted the technology for active wildfires. One August night, drones flew over a carefully selected section of California's nearly million-acre Dixie Fire, dropping incendiary spheres on a mountainside ahead of the advancing flames to start what is known as a backfire. The ignitions slowly walked the intentional burn down the hill, consuming fuel and leaving a fire-unfriendly zone in its wake. Once it reached a distance within 30 feet of a town, ground firefighters could safely put it out to protect homes.

This highly specialized mission is limited by a Federal Aviation Administration rule that requires human operators to be within two miles of most remote-controlled aircraft. Some drone missions are legally required to maintain a line of sight from the operator to the craft. Using autonomous drones would increase the operational distance and provide even greater protection for firefighters, Giles says.

As recent increases in wildfire size and intensity challenge conventional firefighting methods, scientists are also experimenting with groups of remote-controlled aircraft dropping water and other fire-squelching liquids. A swarm of autonomous drones, each capable of carrying a 100-pound payload, could douse flames in a unified assault—so says Elena Ausonio, a professor of mechanical engineering at the University of Genoa, in an April 2021 interview in DroneLife.com. These craft could operate day and night, in heavy smoke and without the need for a nearby water source, Ausonio explained in a recent study she co-wrote.

Other scientists are skeptical about the promise of robotic firefighting technology. "Forest and vegetation management is where immediate efforts should be focused," says Brandon Collins, a fire researcher at University of California, Berkeley. Even scientists immersed in robotic technology admit it is not a magic bullet. Sahota, for example, doubts communities' willingness to invest in robots that can cost in excess of six figures, with each machine designed for very specific needs. "The economies of scale aren't quite the same as [for] mass manufacturing," he says.

Still, as house fires continue to claim human lives and warming temperatures dry out forests, Sahota contends this technology is important for firefighter safety and for straightforward fire suppression. "We don't have enough firefighters as it is," he says. "With climate change, we're already at the breaking point."

About the Author

Jane Braxton Little is an award-winning freelance writer focusing on science and the environment.

The NYPD's Robot Dog Was a Really Bad Idea

By Sophie Bushwick

Editor's Note (4/12/23): On Tuesday New York City mayor Eric Adams announced that the New York City Police Department (NYPD) will be deploying a new fleet of robots and other devices, including the controversial "Digidog." The NYPD first tried out this bot in 2020, but a public backlash to its use led to its retirement in 2021.

In 2020, the New York City Police Department (NYPD) began leasing a caninelike robot—a Spot model from Boston Dynamics that the department nicknamed Digidog. Officers deployed the robot in just a few cases, including a hostage situation in the Bronx and an incident at a public housing building in Manhattan. As word spread (along with photographs and videos), a backlash from the public—and eventually elected officials—quickly gained momentum. Some objected to the robot's expense. Others worried that its use threatened civil liberties. Many simply found it creepy.

The NYPD abruptly terminated its lease and quit using the robot last month. Other U.S. police departments have been testing their own Spot models, however. "Spot has been particularly resourceful in tackling dull, dirty and dangerous tasks," the Boston Dynamics spokesperson told *Scientific American*. "Public safety initiatives, including police departments, often face dangerous work, such as inspecting a bomb, rummaging through remnants of an explosion or fire, or even deescalating a potentially dangerous situation."

Complex social and historical factors influenced the NYPD's decision to pull Digidog from duty. "This is just not a very good time for [the NYPD] to have tried this," says David J. Gunkel, a professor of communication at Northern Illinois University. He notes the department made the move "at a time that we are, as a public, beginning to question what police are doing, how they're being funded and what those monies are being used for." *Scientific American* spoke with Gunkel about why people accept some machines while rejecting others—and whether the public can ever fully accept the idea of robotic cops.

[An edited transcript of the interview follows.]

Q: What influences how we humans feel about robots? People love the cuddly robotic seal PARO, for example, while having a strong negative reaction to Digidog.

A: There's a combination of factors that come into play: the design of the robot, the contexts in which it's deployed and user contributions. The PARO robot is designed to engage humans in more social activities. Boston Dynamics robots are not made to look that way. They don't have a face. They're not furry and cuddly. So design can have an effect on how people respond.

But, also, the context of use is really important. The same Boston Dynamics robots that you saw causing trouble with the New York [City] Police Department, just [a few] years earlier, got a great deal of sympathy from humans. Boston Dynamics engineers were shown kicking the robot. People saw these videos online, and there was this outpouring of emotion for "poor Spot." That robot, because of the context in which it was used, elicited an emotional response that was very different from the response elicited by the police's Digidog robot.

And then, finally, there's what users do with these things. You can design the best robot in the world, but if users don't use it in the way that you've anticipated, that robot could become something very different.

Q: Is there something about robots in particular that makes humans nervous?

A: The really important thing about robots is: they move. And movement is something that elicits, in us human beings, a lot of expectations about what the object is. Already back in the 1940s, [psychologists] Fritz Heider and Marianne Simmel did some studies with very simple animated characters on a piece of film. When they showed this to human test subjects, human

71

beings imparted personality to [a] triangle versus [a] square. And the difference wasn't that the shapes actually had personalities. The difference was the way they moved. Because movement conveys a whole lot of information about social positioning and expectations, the movement of the robots in physical space really carries a great deal of significance for us.

Q: Returning to the public backlash against the NYPD, why did people feel so strongly about this specific robot?

A: It's again a number of factors. One is the very design. The robot, if you've seen pictures of it, is a rather imposing presence. It's a little smaller than the robots you see in science fiction. But the way it navigates through space gives it this very imposing profile that can be seen as creepy by a lot of human observers.

There's also the context of use. The NYPD used this robot, very famously now, [at] a public housing project. That use of the robot in that place, I think, was a really poor choice on the part of the NYPD—because already you're talking about police officers entering a public housing facility, now with this massive technological object, and that [exacerbates the] very big power imbalance that's already there.

Thirdly, there's just timing. This is all taking place in the wake of increased public scrutiny on policing and police practices—especially the militarization of the police—and [how] the police have responded to minority populations in ways that are very different from the way that they have responded to populations of white individuals.

Q: Some people used science fiction to critique Digidog, referencing an episode of the television show *Black Mirror* in which robotic dogs hunted humans. How do stories shape our reaction to technology?

A: The science fiction question is really crucial. We get the word robot from the Czech word *robota*, which comes to us in a stage play from 1920 by Karel Čapek. So our very idea of "robot" is absolutely connected to, and you can't really separate it from, science fiction—because that's where it began.

Also, what the public knows about robots is already predicted in science fiction because we see it in science fiction before we actually see it in social reality. This is called "science-fiction prototyping." Roboticists get some mileage out of it because they can often use science fiction as a way to explain what it is they're building and why. But they also fight [this prototyping] because the science-fiction stories create expectations that inform how people will respond to these things before they ever become social reality. So it's a double-edged sword: it offers opportunities for explanation, but it also inhibits fully understanding what the realities are.

Q: Could the public eventually accept the use of robots in policing?

A: I think this is an evolving scenario. And the decision-making, on the part of police departments, about how these things are integrated or not is going to be crucial. I think you would have seen a very different response had the Digidog robot been used to rescue someone from a fire, as opposed to being brought to a housing project in support of police action. I think you would have seen a very different outcome if it had been used as a bomb-disposal-unit robot. So I think a lot is going to depend not only on the design of the robot but also on the timing of use, the context of use and the positioning of this device with regards to how police interact with their communities—and who they serve.

About the Author

Sophie Bushwick is tech editor at Scientific American. *She runs the daily technology news coverage for the website, writes about everything from artificial intelligence to jumping robots for both digital and print publication, records YouTube and TikTok videos and hosts the podcast* Tech, Quickly. *Bushwick also makes frequent appearances on radio shows such as* Science Friday *and television networks, including* CBS, MSNBC *and* National Geographic. *She has more than a decade of experience as a science journalist based in New York City and previously worked at outlets such as* Popular Science, Discover *and* Gizmodo. *Follow Bushwick on X (formerly Twitter) @sophiebushwick.*

AIs Spot Drones with Help from a Fly Eye

By Monique Brouillette

I n December 2018 thousands of holiday travelers were stranded at London's Gatwick Airport because of reports of drones flying nearby. The airport—one of Europe's busiest—was shut down for two days, which caused major delays and cost airlines millions of dollars. Unauthorized drones in commercial airspace have caused similar incidents in the U.S. and around the world. To stop them, researchers are now developing a detection system inspired by a different type of airborne object: a living fly. This work could have applications far beyond drone detection, researchers write in a paper published in 2022 in the *Journal of the Acoustical Society of America.*

"It's quite awesome," says Frank Ruffier, a researcher at the Etienne-Jules Marey Institute of Movement Sciences at Aix-Marseille University in France and the French National Center for Scientific Research, who was not involved with the new study. "This basic research on the fly is solving a real problem in computer science."

That solution has implications for, among other things, overcoming the inherent difficulty of detecting drones. As these remotely piloted flying machines become ever cheaper and more accessible, many experts worry they will become increasingly disruptive. Their prevalence raises a variety of issues, says Brian Bothwell, co-director of the Science, Technology Assessment and Analytics team at the U.S. Government Accountability Office. "Drones can be operated by both the careless and the criminal," he notes. Careless drone pilots can inadvertently cause accidents; criminal ones can use these devices to smuggle drugs across national borders or drop contraband into prison yards, for example. "It's important to detect them," Bothwell says.

But such detection is far from simple. Current systems rely on visual, auditory or infrared sensors, but these technologies often struggle in conditions that have low visibility, loud noise or interfering signals. Solving the problem requires what computer programmers call "salience detection," which essentially means distinguishing signal from noise.

Now, with some help from nature, a team of scientists and engineers at the University of South Australia, the defense company Midspar Systems and Flinders University in Australia may have found a solution. In their new paper, they demonstrate an algorithm that was designed by reverse engineering the visual system of the hoverfly—a family of mainly black-and-yellow-striped insects known for their habit of hovering around flowers. As anyone who has tried to swat a fly can attest, many of these buzzing pests have incredibly keen vision and fast reaction times. Such abilities stem from their compound eyes, which take in a lot of information simultaneously, and from the neurons that process that information—which turn out to be extremely good at separating relevant signals from meaningless noise. A vast range of animals have visual systems that effectively tune out noise, but the simple brains of flies—and the resulting ease of researching them—make the insects a particularly useful model for computer scientists.

For this study, the researchers examined the hoverfly's visual system to develop a tool that uses similar mechanisms to clean up noisy data. The filtered information can then be fed into an artificial intelligence algorithm for drone detection. In their new paper, the scientists demonstrate that this combination can detect drones up to 50 percent farther away than conventional AI alone. The new research paper is only a proof of concept for the fly-vision algorithm's filtering ability, but the team members have built a prototype and are working toward commercialization. Their efforts demonstrate how bio-inspired design can improve passive detection systems.

"This paper is a great example of how much we potentially can learn from nature about information processing," says Ted Pavlic, associate director of research at Arizona State University's Biomimicry Center, who was not involved in the new study.

To glean insights from the hoverfly, the team spent more than a decade carefully studying the neuronal pathways of its eyes and measuring their electrical responses to light. Starting with the photosensors in the insects' large, compound eyes, the engineers traced the circuits through the various layers of neurons and into the brain. They then used that information to construct an algorithm that can sense and heighten the important parts of the data.

But instead of simply feeding visual data into the algorithm, the researchers fed it spectrograms—visual representations of sound—created from acoustic data recorded in an outdoor environment as drones flew by. The algorithm was able to view these squiggly graphs and heighten the important "signal" peaks that corresponded to frequencies emitted by drones. At the same time, it was able to lessen the background noise that was not created by drones.

"It's really nice because it's a cleaning-up step, and you can basically add it to any machine-learning pipeline and expect to get a benefit from it," says Emma Alexander, a computer scientist at Northwestern University, who was not involved in the study.

In fact, the researchers say they do want to use their bio-inspired algorithm on a variety of applications where artificial intelligence must process information from the real world while dealing with complicated and messy conditions. "We have built a system that can automatically adapt to different environments and enhance the things that are of interest," says study co-author Russell Brinkworth, a biological engineer at Flinders University.

For example, one of the major challenges that comes with building any AI-based sensing system is getting it to work in a constantly changing environment. "In traditional AI, you can't just show it a picture of a car. You have to show it a car in every possible situation in which you could see a car," he explains. "But if the lighting changes or there is a shadow, the AI will say it has never seen it before." This is one of the big hurdles in designing autonomous vehicles that reliably adjust to changing light and other shifting conditions. With the fly-inspired system, however, this filtering happens automatically.

"Artificial intelligence works best when it's in a confined environment and it's controlled," Brinkworth says. "But biology, on the other hand, works everywhere. If it doesn't work everywhere, it dies."

About the Author

Monique Brouillette is a freelance journalist who covers biology. Follow her on X (formerly Twitter) @mo_brouillette.

AI Creates False Documents That Fake Out Hackers

By Sophie Bushwick

Hackers constantly improve at penetrating cyberdefenses to steal valuable documents. So some researchers propose using an artificial-intelligence algorithm to hopelessly confuse them, once they break in, by hiding the real deal amid a mountain of convincing fakes.

The algorithm, called Word Embedding–based Fake Online Repository Generation Engine (WE-FORGE), generates decoys of patents under development. But someday it could "create a lot of fake versions of every document that a company feels it needs to guard," says its developer, Dartmouth College cybersecurity researcher V. S. Subrahmanian.

If hackers were after, say, the formula for a new drug, they would have to find the relevant needle in a haystack of fakes. This could mean checking each formula in detail—and perhaps investing in a few dead-end recipes. "The name of the game here is, 'Make it harder,'" Subrahmanian explains. "'Inflict pain on those stealing from you.'"

Subrahmanian says he tackled this project after reading that companies are unaware of new kinds of cyberattacks for an average of 312 days after they begin. "The bad guy has almost a year to decamp with all our documents, all our intellectual property," he says. "Even if you're a Pfizer, that's enough time to steal almost everything. It's not just the crown jewels—it's the crown jewels, and the jewels of the maid, and the watch of the secretary!"

Counterfeit documents produced by WE-FORGE could also act as hidden "trip wires," says Rachel Tobac, CEO of cybersecurity consultancy SocialProof Security. For example, an enticing file might alert security when accessed. Companies have typically used human-created fakes for this strategy. "But now if this AI is able to do that for us, then we can create a lot of new documents that are believable for an attacker—without having to do more work," says Tobac, who was not involved in the project.

The system produces convincing decoys by searching through a document for keywords. For each one it finds, it calculates a list of related concepts and replaces the original term with one chosen at random. The process can produce dozens of documents that contain no proprietary information but still look plausible. Subrahmanian and his team asked computer science and chemistry graduate students to evaluate real and fake patents from their respective fields, and the humans found the WE-FORGE-generated documents highly believable. The results appeared in the Association for Computing Machinery's *Transactions on Management Information Systems*.

WE-FORGE might eventually expand its scope, but Subrahmanian notes that a document recommending a course of action, for instance, would be much more complex than a technical formula. Still, both he and Tobac think this research will attract commercial interest. "I could definitely see an organization leveraging this type of product," Tobac says. "If this … creates believable decoys without releasing sensitive details within those decoys, then I think you've got a huge win there."

About the Author

Sophie Bushwick is tech editor at Scientific American. *She runs the daily technology news coverage for the website, writes about everything from artificial intelligence to jumping robots for both digital and print publication, records YouTube and TikTok videos and hosts the podcast* Tech, Quickly. *Bushwick also makes frequent appearances on radio shows such as* Science Friday *and television networks, including* CBS, MSNBC *and* National Geographic. *She has more than a decade of experience as a science journalist based in New York City and previously worked at outlets such as* Popular Science, Discover *and* Gizmodo. *Follow Bushwick on X (formerly Twitter) @sophiebushwick.*

AI's Climate Impact Goes beyond Its Emissions

By Jude Coleman

Artificial intelligence is not limited to entertaining chatbots: increasingly effective programs trained with machine learning have become integral to uses ranging from smartphone GPS navigators to the algorithms that govern social media. But as AI's popularity keeps rising, more researchers and experts are noting the environmental cost. Training and running an AI system requires a great deal of computing power and electricity, and the resulting carbon dioxide emissions are one way AI affects the climate. But its environmental impact goes well beyond its carbon footprint.

"It is important for us to recognize the CO_2 emissions of some of these large AI systems especially," says Jesse Dodge, a research scientist at the Allen Institute for AI in Seattle. He adds, however, that "the impact of AI systems in general is going to be from the applications they're built for, not necessarily the cost of training."

The exact effect that AI will have on the climate crisis is difficult to calculate, even if experts focus only on the amount of greenhouse gases it emits. That's because different types of AI—such as a machine learning model that spots trends in research data, a vision program that helps self-driving cars avoid obstacles or a large language model (LLM) that enables a chatbot to converse—all require different quantities of computing power to train and run. For example, when OpenAI trained its LLM called GPT-3, that work produced the equivalent of around 500 tons of carbon dioxide. Simpler models, though, produce minimal emissions. Further complicating the matter, there's a lack of transparency from many AI companies, Dodge says. That makes it even more complicated to understand their models' impact—when they are examined only through an emissions lens.

This is one reason experts increasingly recommend treating AI's emissions as only one aspect of its climate footprint. David Rolnick, a computer scientist at McGill University, likens AI to a hammer: "The primary impact of a hammer is what is being hammered," he says, "not what is in the hammer." Just as the tool can smash things to bits or pound in nails to build a house, artificial intelligence can hurt or help the environment.

Take the fossil-fuel industry. In 2019 Microsoft announced a new partnership with ExxonMobil and stated that the company would use Microsoft's cloud-computing platform Azure. The oil giant claimed that by using the technology—which relies on AI for certain tasks such as performance analysis—it could optimize mining operations and, by 2025, increase production by 50,000 oil-equivalent barrels per day. (An oil-equivalent barrel is a term used to compare different fuel sources—it's a unit roughly equal to the energy produced by burning one barrel of crude oil.) In this case, Microsoft's AI is directly used to add more fossil fuels, which will release greenhouse gases when burned, to the market.

In a statement emailed to *Scientific American*, a Microsoft spokesperson said the company believes that "technology has an important role to play in helping the industry decarbonize, and this work must move forward in a principled manner—balancing the energy needs and industry practices of today while inventing and deploying those of tomorrow." The spokesperson added that the company sells its technology and cloud services to "all customers, inclusive of energy customers."

Fossil-fuel extraction is not the only AI application that could be environmentally harmful. "There's examples like this across every sector, like forestry, land management, farming," says Emma Strubell, a computer scientist at Carnegie Mellon University.

This can also be seen in the way AI is used in automated advertising. When an eerily specific ad pops up on your Instagram or Facebook news feed, advertising algorithms are the wizard behind the curtain. This practice boosts overall consumptive behavior in society, Rolnick says. For instance, with fast-fashion advertising, targeted ads push a steady rotation of cheap, mass-produced clothes to consumers, who buy the outfits only to replace them as soon as a new trend arrives. That creates a higher demand for fast-fashion companies, and already the fashion industry is collectively estimated to produce up to eight percent of global emissions. Fast fashion produces yet more emissions from shipping and causes more discarded clothes to pile up in landfills. Meta, the parent company of Instagram and Facebook, did not respond to *Scientific American*'s request for comment.

But on the other side of the coin there are AI applications that can help deal with climate change and other environmental problems, such as the destruction wrought by severe heat-fueled hurricanes. One such application is xView2, a program that combines machine-learning models and computer vision with satellite imagery to identify buildings damaged in natural disasters. The program was launched by the Defense Innovation Unit, a U.S. Department of Defense organization. Its models can assess damaged infrastructure, thereby reducing danger and saving time for first responders who would otherwise have to make those assessments themselves. It can also help search-and-rescue teams more quickly identify where to direct their efforts.

Other AI technologies can be applied directly to climate change mitigation by using them to monitor emissions. "In the majority of the world, for the majority of climate change emissions, it's very opaque," says Gavin McCormick, executive director of WattTime, a company that monitors electricity-related emissions. WattTime is a founding partner of the nonprofit organization Climate TRACE, whose platform combines computer vision and machine learning to flag emissions from global pollution sources. First, scientists identify the emissions coming from monitored facilities. Then they use satellite imagery to pinpoint visual signs of the emission-causing activities—steam plumes from a factory, for example. Next, engineers train algorithms on those data in order to teach the programs to estimate emissions based on visual input alone. The resulting numbers can then help corporations determine to lower their emissions footprint, can inform policymakers and can hold polluters accountable.

As AI becomes more efficient at solving environmental problems, such as by helping to lower emissions, it could prove to be a valuable tool in the fight against climate change—if the AI industry can reduce its negative climate impacts. "From the policy standpoint, both AI policy and climate policy have roles to play," Rolnick says. In particular he recommends shaping AI policy in a way that considers all angles of its impact on climate. That means looking at its applications as well as its emissions and other production costs, such as those from water use.

Further, Dodge adds that those with expertise in AI, particularly people in power at tech companies, should establish ethical principles to limit the technology's use. The goal should be to avoid climate harm and instead help reduce it. "It needs to be part of the value system," he says.

About the Author

Jude Coleman is an Oregon-based freelance science journalist who covers stories about ecology, climate change and the environment.

Elon Musk's Neuralink Has Implanted Its First Chip in a Human Brain

By Ben Guarino

Billionaire technologist Elon Musk announced in January 2024 that his company Neuralink has implanted its brain-computer interface into a human for the first time. The recipient was "recovering well," Musk wrote on his social media platform X (formerly Twitter) on Monday evening, adding that initial results showed "promising neuron spike detection"—a reference to brain cells' electrical activity.

Each wireless Neuralink device contains a chip and electrode arrays of more than 1,000 superthin, flexible conductors that a surgical robot threads into the cerebral cortex. There the electrodes are designed to register thoughts related to motion. In Musk's vision, an app will eventually translate these signals to move a cursor or produce text—in short, it will enable computer control by thinking. "Imagine if Stephen Hawking could communicate faster than a speed typist or auctioneer. That is the goal," Musk wrote of the first Neuralink product, which he said is named Telepathy.

The U.S. Food and Drug Administration had approved human clinical trials for Neuralink in May 2023. And last September the company announced it was opening enrollment in its first study to people with quadriplegia.

Musk's announcement did not take neuroscientists by surprise. Musk, the world's richest man, "said he was going to do it," says John Donoghue, an expert in brain-computer interfaces at Brown University. "He had done the preliminary work, built on the shoulders of others, including what we did starting in the early 2000s."

Neuralink's original ambitions, which Musk outlined when he founded the company in 2016, included meshing human brains with artificial intelligence. Its more immediate aims seem in line with the neural keyboards and other devices that people with paralysis already use to operate computers. The methods and speed with which Neuralink pursued those goals, however, have resulted in federal investigations into dead study animals and the transportation of hazardous material.

Musk has a habit of suggesting big things but providing little detail, notes Ryan Merkley, director of research advocacy at the Physicians Committee for Responsible Medicine. "This is maybe the biggest example of that" because there's no information available about the person who received the implant or their medical condition, Merkley points out. "Depending on the patient's disease or disorder, success can look very different."

Scientific American spoke with Donoghue to understand what the latest step signifies for Neuralink—and whether the company might ever achieve Musk's more extreme goals.

[An edited transcript of the interview follows.]

Q: In describing the first results, Musk used the phrase "promising neuron spike detection." What might that mean?

A: I have to preface this by saying that, as a scientist, you can't comment on anything until you have a paper in hand. But what that generally means is: there are action potentials [the electrical impulses that nerve cells create], and there's a probe in the brain, and it's picking up signals that are there.

But I have to remain open to what that actually means. I have to see the data. And commercial entities do this piecemeal-feeding things. The danger with that, of course, is: tomorrow it may stop working.

Q: Are you concerned by how the recent information on this trial was drip fed on a social media platform or anything else about how the research has been communicated to scientists or the public?

A: I don't particularly like it, but I don't want to overstate that.... It's legitimate to say you implanted someone. I don't think they want to say much about what it means or what it does.

Q: From where you're sitting, what can Neuralink bring to the table beyond the research that you and others have done—for instance, your work on enabling a participant to move a computer cursor on a screen by thought? Does Neuralink have the opportunity to do something different?

A: They're a commercial entity, right? They want a product. When I started, I had a company called Cyberkinetics, which was too early. [Cyberkinetics was acquired in 2008 by what is now Blackrock Neurotech.] One of the differences is something on the order of $100 million. In those days, we lacked all the money and the knowledge. Now we have the knowledge. [Musk has] put in the money.

What he's done is taken in investments, taken all that knowledge that the field has created. Certainly [that means research done by] not just us but [also] lots of [other] people, basic scientists who have figured out how the motor cortex works, including us but definitely not exclusively us, [as well as neuroscientists] Apostolos Georgopoulos, Andy Schwartz—all those people built a foundation. He could take all that knowledge and put the money in to create the kind of product that could potentially be commercial, though that's yet to be determined.

I'm really happy to see that there will be (likely, we'll see what happens with this particular version) a commercial product that will someday reach people and help them.

Q: In terms of Neuralink's approach, what's novel about having a chip talk wirelessly to a device versus other proof-of-principle lab demonstrations? Previous implants have captured signals from individual neurons, but this may require cables to transmit the large amount of data involved.

A: That's an important step to get everything inside. The problem has been that it's a lot of information. And they came up with a solution that was more practical than I was thinking. I was hoping to get [a] full-bandwidth, high rate of information.

They're using Bluetooth, which is a much reduced version.... But they get enough information to be able to control things.

With the information they take out, they're not able to pull apart every single neuron out of the whole mess. They mix things together a little bit, because the bandwidth doesn't allow them to sort out everything. But it works.

Q: After this announcement, are we any closer to Musk's loftier goals? He has talked about restoring eyesight to people who are blind and mobility to those who are disabled and even about this wild AI-merging scenario.

A: Somebody asked [bioengineer] Ed Maynard, who was my graduate student in 1999, exactly that kind of question. He said, "We have modest goals: we want to make blind people see, paralyzed people move and deaf people hear again." So that's an old line that's been kicking around for 25 years. And of course, everything we do toward improving the ability for people to have these things makes us a step closer to helping paralyzed people communicate and move again in a practical way, [with a] commercial device.

The thing is, you've got to be careful. The whole nature of restoring sensory inputs, like vision, involves electrical stimulation in the brain. It's a whole different ball game. It's not recording from single cells—that's one thing—it's stimulation.

And as far as I know, there's not one scintilla of evidence of using that device to create sensory systems in any way. It's a whole other project. You could say, "You've got a car. Do you think [a boat] will work?" Who knows? Yeah, it could, but it's not a car.

They would need to outline what they think are the steps. Can you put electrodes in the brain? Yes. Can they stay in there? Yes. Can you stimulate them? I don't know—they're supposed to be able to. Can you stimulate them in the right way? Vision has been very complicated in terms of putting electrodes into the brain and trying to restore a meaningful image.

Q: Are there limits to what a brain-computer interface can offer? Is it beyond the motivation that Musk has stated? Do we still have that dream of what folks were talking about 25 years ago?

A: The nature of science is: you never know what's around the corner. I'm sure you saw *Oppenheimer*.

Q: Yeah.

A: There were two potential outcomes of that [first detonation of an atomic bomb]: you'd get a really big boom, or you'd destroy Earth if it didn't stop. They didn't know. We don't know! There are lots of things that have happened that I wouldn't have ever predicted. The use of communication is much better than I thought it would ever be.

The engineering stuff is: Will we get a low-power amplifier that's much smaller, that will have more bandwidth? Almost certainly, but you're not talking to an expert in that area. It looks to me like we're getting better and better with the capabilities of electronics. The engineers can tell us, "These are not insurmountable problems." We have the technology already. And then there are other things that are going to be hard to do. They're scientific questions [for which] I have no idea what the answer will be until we do the experiments.

About the Author

Ben Guarino is an associate technology editor at Scientific American. *He writes and edits stories about artificial intelligence, robotics and our relationship with our tools. Previously, he worked as a science editor at* Popular Science *and a staff writer at the* Washington Post, *where he covered the COVID pandemic, science policy and misinformation (and also dinosaur bones and water bears). He has a degree in bioengineering from the University of Pennsylvania and a master's degree from New York University's Science, Health and Environmental Reporting Program.*

Section 4: Getting Around

Future Space Travel Might Require Mushrooms

By Nick Hilden

The list of mycologists whose names are known beyond their fungal field is short, and at its apex is Paul Stamets. Educated in, and a longtime resident of, the mossy, moldy, mushy Pacific Northwest region, Stamets has made numerous contributions over the past several decades—perhaps the best summation of which can be found in his 2005 book *Mycelium Running: How Mushrooms Can Help Save the World*. But now he is looking beyond Earth to discover new ways that mushrooms can help with the exploration of space.

In a new "astromycological" venture launched in conjunction with NASA, Stamets and various research teams are studying how fungi can be leveraged to build extraterrestrial habitats and perhaps someday even terraform planets. This is not the first time Stamets's career has intersected with speculative space science. He also recently received an honor that many researchers would consider only slightly less hallowed than a Nobel Prize: the distinction of having a *Star Trek* character named after him.

Scientific American spoke with Stamets about the out-of-this-world implications for the emerging field of astromycology.

[An edited transcript of the interview follows.]

Q: First, a chicken-or-egg question: Did *Star Trek: Discovery* name a character after you because you had started exploring astromycology, or was the idea for astromycology inspired by *Star Trek*?

A: CBS got ahold of me and said the writers of *Star Trek* wanted to talk to me: "We're in the dungeon, there's about a dozen of us, we've been tasked with *Star Trek: Discovery*, we're hitting a brick wall, and we saw your TED Talk." I had mentioned terraforming other planets with fungi.

What separates *Star Trek* from other science fiction, you know, is it really pioneered the importance of inclusivity, recognizing that the diversity of the members of our society gives us strength. And, indeed, that's what I've learned as a mycologist: the biodiversity of our ecosystem gives our ecosystem resilience. Ultimately, diversity wins.

So I told them terraforming with fungi on other planets is very plausible. Fungi were the first organisms that came to land, munching rocks, and fungi gave birth to animals about 650 million years ago. We're descendants of the descendants of these fungal networks.

I said, "You can have all these concepts for free. I'm a *Star Trek* fan; I don't want anything for this." I said, "But, you know, I always wanted to be the first astromycologist." And at the very end, they go, "Astromycologist, we love that! What a great phrase; we can use that."

Q: How do you define the term astromycology here in our nonfictional universe?

A: Astromycology is obviously a subset of astrobiology, so astrobiology would be the study of biological organisms extraterrestrially.

Really, you're talking about the biology of the universe—and within the biology of the universe is our fungi. So astromycology would be the study of fungal biology throughout the universe. And I think it's inevitable we're going to someday find fungi on other planets.

Q: How can Earth's fungi help with the development of human habitats or even entire ecosystems on other planets?

A: [Plants that support terraforming] need minerals, and pairing fungi up with the plants and debris from humans [causes them to] decompose into a form that then creates rich soils that could help generate the foods that astronauts need. It's much easier to take one seed and grow your food than it is to take a ton of food to space, right? Nature is incredibly efficient in terms of a payload. It's much better for nature to generate a payload of food than for your rocket to carry a payload of food.

Q: Your current research proposal with NASA has two stages. The first involves identifying the best fungal species for breaking down asteroid regolith. Do you currently have any possible candidates?

A: Basically, regolith is asteroid dust. [Research teams] have constructed [synthetic] regolith that is supposed to mimic the components that are found on the surface of asteroids and also on Mars. So we're working with them now. I have a suite of about 700 strains of fungi in my cultural library. I made some recommendations, and I'm happy to say oyster mushrooms are one of the best ones that we've experimented with on the regolith so far.

And just recently we have found something synergistically that was unexpected when we took one species, gave it a nutritional source, and we wanted to know how far it would grow into the regolith [with its mycelial roots]. When we took one species of fungi, and we looked at the reach that it had in the regolith, then we combined it with other species of fungi— each of which did not have that great of a reach. When we had a plurality of fungal species together, the outreach was far greater than anticipated. In some ways, it just proves this whole concept about biodiversity.

Q: The second stage [headed by astrobiologist Lynn Rothschild and her team at NASA Ames] involves determining the most effective way to use a fungus once the best type is selected. What might that look like?

A: The universe is rich with hydrocarbons. What oyster mushrooms do really well is break down hydrocarbons and dismantle them and restructure them into fungal carbohydrates, into sugars. Sugars are an absolutely essential nutrient, of course, for practically all life forms that I know of on this planet. So the idea of using hydrocarbons as a feedstock for oyster mushrooms makes a lot of sense.

Now, you have these kind of start/stops. You can only go so far without other inputs of essential nutrients. So it's not like the fungi could just use hydrocarbons alone—they need a boost. That's where we have to supplement them. But once you begin to create this reaction, it becomes catalytic—that is, self-sustaining. The more you feed this catalytic reaction, the more biodiversity you have. Again, you are having other organisms grow and die. They become a resource that provides vitamins, other minerals, perhaps other decomposable organic compounds such as cellulose or lignin, which can fuel these fungi to grow even larger and then support more plants that create more cellulose. And then they die, and they decompose, and these lenses of mycelium—shallow, usually circular colonies of mycelium—then begin to grow out more and more. So you're creating a micro-oasis environment that may just be a speck. And then these things begin to elaborate. And as their communities become more diverse and complex, these lenses of life then begin to become larger oases. And when the oasis environment is large enough, then it can sustain humans.

Q: **In addition to generating healthy soil, there are teams investigating how fungi might be used to grow structures on other worlds. Could you tell me more about how this sort of so-called mycotecture might work?**

A: We grow lots of reishi mycelium, for instance. We grow reishi blocks. We wanted to crush these blocks in order to turn them into soil or get other value-added products. So we dried out these reishi blocks and we tried to crush them. But we *couldn't* crush them. You could saw them with a saw blade, but if you tried to hit them with a hammer or something, they just wouldn't break. So this great engineer built us a hydraulic stainless steel press, and I had like 2,000 psi [pounds per square inch] in this press, and we gave it my reishi blocks, and it bent the stainless steel. Trying to compress it, it actually broke the machine. This thing will crush rocks all day long and could not crush mycelium.

They're so structurally strong. They're also good at retaining heat, so their insulation properties are phenomenal. Moreover, these could become batteries. You can have solar panels on a structure on Mars made of mycelium. (The entire mycelium is about 85 percent carbon, and studies have shown that porous carbon can be an excellent capacitor.) You could then pregrow these and arrange them on a form such that they become nanobatteries. And they could then not only insulate you from the cold on the Martian or asteroid surface, but the house itself becomes a giant battery for power because they're so rich in carbon fibers. So that, to me, is really cool.

Q: What kind of timelines do you have in mind for all of this? Is this the sort of thing we might see applied a decade from now or in a century?

A: Tomorrow. It's happening now. I'm guessing it will be implemented in space within 10 to 20 years.

Q: Before we wrap up, let's get a little more speculative. What are some of the more fantastic ways mushrooms might be applied in space?

A: Well, what I can tell you? I'm sure some of your editors may go, "No way, we're not going to publish this." But I think using psilocybin mushrooms in spaceflight makes a lot of sense. There are more than 65 articles right now ... at ClinicalTrials.gov that say psilocybin mushrooms help people overcome [post-traumatic stress disorder], loneliness and depression. Do you think the astronauts are going to have loneliness and depression and PTSD? I think yes. How are you going to help them?

Under carefully controlled conditions, our astronauts [being] able to take psilocybin in space and look at the universe and not feel distant and alone but feel like they're part of this giant consciousness will give them a better frame of mind—

psychologically, emotionally—to work with other astronauts and stay on mission. I feel that isolation, loneliness and depression are going to be major issues that astronauts face.

So I say this with great sincerity: NASA and anyone else working and looking at the settlement of space, you should consider that psilocybin mushrooms should be an essential part of your psychological tool kit for astronauts to be able to endure the solitude and the challenges of space and isolation.

Psilocybin mushrooms build creativity; people who are more creative come up with more solutions. I think that, in a sense, is a fertile ecosystem that can lead to the sustainability of humans in space.

About the Author

Nick Hilden writes for the likes of the Washington Post, Esquire, Popular Science, National Geographic, *the* Daily Beast, *and more. You can follow him on X (formerly Twitter) @nickhilden or Instagram @nick.hilden.*

Rotating Sails Help to Revive Wind-Powered Shipping

By Lynn Freehill-Maye

In 1926 a cargo ship called the *Buckau* crossed the Atlantic sporting what looked like two tall smokestacks. But these towering cylinders were actually drawing power from the wind. Called Flettner rotors, they were a surprising new invention by German engineer Anton Flettner (covered at the time in *Scientific American*). When the wind was perpendicular to the ship's course, a motor spun the cylinders so their forward-facing sides turned in the same direction as the wind; this movement made air move faster across the front surface and slower behind, creating a pressure difference and pulling the ship forward. The rotating sails provided a net energy gain—but before they could be widely adopted the Great Depression struck, followed by World War II. Like the electric car, the Flettner rotor would be abandoned for almost a century in favor of burning fossil fuel.

Now, with shippers under renewed pressure to cut both costs and carbon emissions, the concept is getting shot. In one notable example, the 12,000-gross-ton cargo vessel *SC Connector* is adding 35-meter Flettner rotors that can tilt to near horizontal when the ship passes under bridges or power lines. The new rotors need electrical power to spin, but manufacturer Norsepower says they can still save up to 20 percent on fuel consumption and cut emissions by 25 percent.

The *SC Connector* is one of a growing series of rotor-boosted ships expected to be operating in various parts of the world by year's end, according to SSPA, a Sweden-based nonprofit research institute. Shipbuilders are also incorporating other wind-propulsion technologies, such as kite-style sails. But Flettner rotors are getting the earliest adoption, says Sofia Werner, a naval architect who leads an SSPA team studying their performance. Ships can easily be retrofitted, literally overnight, with rotors activated by an on/off switch. "It's a quite simple solution, understandable and safe," Werner says. "It's also very visible, which is good for marketing."

The United Nations International Maritime Organization has set ambitious decarbonization goals involving marine fuels, and the European Union is now funding rotor research. Climate pressures and easy installation make wind-power systems an attractive option, according to the International Windship Association. "A lot of people wanted to see wind dead [in the 1920s] because they were making a lot of money off fuel," says Gavin Allwright, the organization's secretary-general. "That's still true today. I can't sell you a unit of wind. What I am bullish about is that where we've got a major decarbonization issue, [alternative fuels] have great potential but are five to 10 years from being proven out. Wind, we could put on a vessel today."

Will Trackless Trams Gain Traction in the U.S.?

By Sophie Bushwick

Joe Ciresi used to drive about 30 miles into Philadelphia for work every day. "It took anywhere from an hour and a half to three hours, depending on traffic," he recounts. "I said, 'This is insanity.'" Now a Pennsylvania state representative, Ciresi has been thinking about how to reduce the number of cars on the road. Recently he and his staff were looking at public transport options and encountered a video about trackless trams created by Peter Newman, a researcher at the Curtin University Sustainability Policy Institute in Perth, Australia.

Public transportation is essential to reducing gridlock and emissions on highways and in cities, Newman says. But trains require extensive infrastructure spending, and historically buses have been unpopular because of potentially bumpy and traffic-slowed rides. Now, however, new technology can let buslike vehicles run on roads for a ride resembling the more popular experience of rail travel—without rails. Newman describes one example already running in China: a self-driving electric bus with optical sensors that let it follow a white line painted on the road. Its hydraulic suspension system, a type often used in trains, eases jolts.

"What impressed me in China was that the ride quality was ... equivalent to what I had experienced on a modern light rail, where everything is fixed on a steel track," Newman says. To emphasize the technological advances making these souped-up buses more pleasant to ride, Newman advocates officially calling them "trackless trams." He is working to bring them to Perth and says they are being studied or tried out in Zimbabwe and Qatar. "I think you'll find that in the next decade [the idea will] take off very quickly," he says.

Trackless trams avoid the need for expensive rail systems, but they do require some changes to infrastructure. "Most of the cost of these new systems that we're building is in that cost of constructing the right of way," says Yale Wong, a transportation researcher at the University of Sydney. In Ciresi's area of Pennsylvania, for example, creating a dedicated trackless tram lane would mean modifying about a dozen overpasses for the specialized vehicles. Wong notes that these changes could also support a dedicated bus route—but "people just don't like buses." He suggests that a form of transit associated with rails (and with shiny new technology) has a better chance of earning the public's enthusiasm.

That is why Ciresi hopes to demonstrate trackless trams in the U.S. before pushing for infrastructure changes. "We do a test run, maybe for five miles ... and we find out if this is worth the investment," he says. "I think, as Americans, we like to see the product and be able to hold, touch, feel and give our opinion of it."

About the Author

Sophie Bushwick is tech editor at Scientific American. *She runs the daily technology news coverage for the website, writes about everything from artificial intelligence to jumping robots for both digital and print publication, records YouTube and TikTok videos and hosts the podcast* Tech, Quickly. *Bushwick also makes frequent appearances on radio shows such as Science Friday and television networks, including CBS, MSNBC and National Geographic. She has more than a decade of experience as a science journalist based in New York City and previously worked at outlets such as* Popular Science, Discover *and* Gizmodo. *Follow Bushwick on X (formerly Twitter) @sophiebushwick.*

Better Bus Systems Could
Slow Climate Change

By Kendra Pierre-Louis

For the past decade Seattle has been growing—fast. Between 2010 and 2020 its population swelled by almost a quarter. Growth is generally good for cities, but it is often accompanied by a dreaded problem: traffic. Yet Seattle managed to avert this crisis, cutting traffic in its downtown by 10 percent and reducing greenhouse gas emissions in the process. How did Seattle do it? By turning to an uncommon solution: the humble bus.

Buses are among the most overlooked solutions for decarbonizing the U.S. Transportation is the single largest source of greenhouse gas emissions, making up slightly less than 30 percent, according to the Environmental Protection Agency. In the summer of 2022 more than 5 percent of new auto sales in the U.S. were for all-electric vehicles (EVs), signaling that electric-car ownership had shifted from being a fad of early adopters to a transportation staple. Three of the four car commercials that aired during the 2023 Super Bowl were for EVs. In January, President Joe Biden tweeted, "On my watch, the great American road trip is going to be fully electrified," alongside a photograph of himself behind the wheel of an electric Hummer.

The president has supported EVs as part of the nation's climate plan, pledging to reduce emissions by 50 to 52 percent by 2030. This commitment is in line with the aims of the Paris Agreement. But Steven Higashide, director of the Clean Transportation program at the Union of Concerned Scientists, cautions that "electrifying personal vehicles is necessary but not sufficient" for achieving the nation's goals on climate change reduction.

A growing body of research bolsters his point. A 2018 report by the California Air Resources Board found that the state could not meet its 2030 climate goals through vehicle electrification alone. At the time, California aimed to reduce greenhouse gas emissions to 40 percent of the state's 1990 levels by 2030. But according to the report, even if there were 10 times as many EVs on the road, people would still need to reduce their driving by 25 percent for California to reach its target.

The culprit is something known as vehicle fleet turnover—that is, how long it takes to shift the mix of vehicles that are on the road. Even if every new vehicle sold from now on were electric and directly replaced a gas-powered car, it would still be at least 15 years before virtually every car on the road was electric. But sales of new gas cars are still higher than those of EVs, which is why even the more ambitious estimates say roughly a third of cars will still be gas in 2050.

Even if the U.S. could somehow avoid the fleet-turnover problem, swapping gas cars one-for-one with EVs would create new energy needs requiring half of the country's electricity-generating capacity, according to a 2020 analysis in the journal *Nature Climate Change*. This demand would limit the nation's ability to power other things such as air-conditioning that are necessary for health and safety in a warming world. To meet the country's climate goals, Higashide says we'll have to drive less frequently and for shorter distances—and redesign cities and neighborhoods with good mass transit options.

Buses can fill a lot of those needs. It's better if they're powered by electric batteries, but even gas buses reduce emissions with enough riders. On average, cars emit almost one pound of carbon dioxide per passenger mile. Buses, which generally run at about 25 percent capacity, emit 0.64 pound of CO_2 per passenger mile, according to data from the Department of Defense. If they ran full, buses would emit 0.18 pound of CO_2 per passenger mile, making them comparable to rail but at a much lower cost. "I think the bus is often overlooked as a climate solution," Higashide says, "because it is overlooked as a solution, period."

Converting Drivers to Riders

Buses have long been maligned in popular imagination. In movies and television shows, scriptwriters often have characters ride the bus to telegraph to viewers that they are facing tough times. On the HBO series *Insecure*, main character Issa Dee's downward spiral begins with her crashing her car and having to ride the bus. In the ultimate bus flick, *Speed*, Annie is on the bus because her driver's license has been revoked—for speeding. Why else would a nice girl like her be riding the bus in Los Angeles?

It would seem that buses are a hard sell in a country that loves the automobile, but research suggests that isn't necessarily true. According to a 2016 analysis led by Higashide that looked at transit-ridership behavior among both car owners and those without cars, people who live near better transit ride it more often regardless of whether they own a vehicle. The problem is that many Americans do not live near better transit. An analysis by the American Society of Civil Engineers found that 45 percent of people in the U.S. lack access to transit at all. Those who do have transit available find it is often slow and unreliable.

The amount of time between buses or trains at a given stop, known as headway, has a huge impact on whether people will actually use the service. "Ten minutes is that magic mark," says Kari Watkins, an associate professor of civil and environmental engineering at the University of California, Davis. Watkins's research looks at how to expand mobility through methods other than driving. When a bus arrives every 10 minutes or less, riders don't have to think about when the bus is coming. This experience mirrors the main convenience of private car ownership: transportation is available when you need it.

When buses arrive every 15 or 20 minutes, "people are still going to feel like they have to time their trips," Watkins says. Past that, "anybody who has a choice is not as likely to opt for transit." Buses that arrive with an unpredictable cadence because of traffic and other factors also turn people away.

In this way, trains have some benefits over buses because they run on a fixed schedule. The two modes are probably best used in a complementary way: rail can carry large numbers of people in denser communities, and buses can serve to funnel people to those rail lines. Even in New York City—a place well known for its subway system—buses shuttle more than one million riders daily. Buses are also much nimbler than trains because they leverage an existing piece of infrastructure: the road. Routes can be adjusted to meet shifting needs, whereas train tracks cannot be moved.

Yet "in many parts of the country, there has been an investment in rail without the corresponding investment in bus service," Higashide says. He points to Denver: the city has spent billions expanding its light rail and commuter rail systems, but "then you get off the train, and the bus comes every hour."

David King, a planning professor at Arizona State University, thinks transit service, especially bus transit, is so poor in the U.S. partly because it's treated as a social or public service—a form of government support or assistance for disadvantaged people. Nationwide, transit riders are more likely to have lower incomes than drivers, and among people who ride, those who take the train tend to have higher incomes than bus passengers. Bus riders are more likely to be people with no other option.

"We usually call them transit-dependent riders," says Candace Brakewood, an associate professor in the department of civil and environmental engineering at the University of Tennessee, Knoxville. "They often are low income, can't afford a car or perhaps have a disability, and can't drive or really don't want to drive." Research shows, however, that if service is bad enough, even those who are ostensibly transit-dependent will find other ways of getting around, such as walking, biking, hitching rides and using informal transit networks.

In many cities, buses are treated as critical infrastructure. Take Bogotá, Colombia, for instance, which has no metro service and has roughly the same size population as New York City. The bus rapid transit system, TransMilenio, has priority lanes that shuttle passengers faster than private cars during peak traffic periods. Sleek, well-lit stations were carefully planned to be accessible by sidewalk as well as by bicycle. It's estimated that immediately after launching in 2000, TransMilenio helped to cut air pollution by as much as 40 percent in certain locales, reduced car fatalities by 92 percent, and even seduced some commuters into giving up their cars—11 percent of riders identify as former drivers.

Higashide points out that when transit is safe, reliable and fast, like it is with TransMilenio, it can feel like a public luxury. That term, whose recent popularity traces back to writer and activist George Monbiot, refers to services and experiences that feel luxurious but are intended for public consumption. Instead of private pools, it's public pools that are clean, properly staffed and open during the hours when you'd actually like to go. It's big, keystone parks such as Griffith Park in Los Angeles and Central Park in New York, but it's also the well-tended neighborhood playground with swings that glide effortlessly. At its core, public luxury is the idea that "the good stuff" doesn't have to be locked up in private ownership. Owning a car, after all, comes with its own set of headaches. A bus system like TransMilenio makes choosing transit over driving almost pleasurable rather than a sacrifice.

In addition to running fast and frequently, a bus system that feels like a public luxury will have routes that take riders to the places they want to go (the movies, a friend's house, a museum), as well as the places they need to go (work, the doctor's office). Bus stops will be well marked in safe locations, with seating and protection from sun and rain.

Because most riders get to bus stops by walking, sidewalks and other surrounding infrastructure are needed, too. In 2011 a child in Georgia was killed by a hit-and-run driver while he and his family were crossing the street to get to their bus stop. The stop was located directly across from their apartment complex, but crossing the street via the nearest crosswalk would have meant walking an additional two thirds of a mile.

Well-designed bus systems allow people who can't drive or simply don't want to—such as older people and people with certain disabilities—to get around. They also enable older children and teens who are too young to drive to transport themselves from home to school and to extracurricular activities on their own, freeing up parents' time. And riders tend to have a special relationship with buses in part because of their drivers. "If you're doing a trip regularly, it's nice to know the person you're traveling with," Watkins says. It's the feeling that "they're looking out for you."

Better Buses, Better Cities

Beyond emissions, there are other reasons to want fewer people driving. In addition to the climate crisis, we also have "a justice crisis, a safety crisis and an economic crisis, all of which come together on our roadways," King says. Their solutions, he adds, can come from the roadways, too.

It's no mystery that significant investment is needed to make bus transit viable. In 2022 Antelope Valley in northeastern California became the first municipality to unveil an all-electric bus fleet. The upgrade cost roughly $80 million, or about $1 million per bus. But the Antelope Valley Transit Authority notes that the upgrades came with savings—the electric fleet's first 10 million miles saved the agency $3.3 million in avoided fuel costs. The new buses also emitted 59 million fewer pounds of CO_2 over the same distance.

Municipalities aren't the only ones saving money. Cars have long been considered a ticket to the middle class partly because it's difficult to find work in most places without one. On average, Americans spend about 13 percent of their income on transportation; those with the lowest incomes spend nearly 30 percent. Nationwide, car debt totals more than $1.4 trillion and is projected to grow. Buses can reduce economic pressures and increase access to opportunity.

Fewer drivers on the road will also save lives. More than 40,000 people are killed in motor vehicle crashes every year in the

U.S. Compared with their gas counterparts, EVs are heavier and can accelerate faster.

Political will—the risk of angering drivers by giving up public roadways to public transit in particular—is often the biggest hurdle to implementing changes. But Seattle has shown it can be done. "King County Metro in Seattle had a whole group dedicated to speed and reliability," Watkins says. Between 2010 and 2017 the city's ridership grew, bucking nationwide trends that saw bus ridership decline by 15 percent between 2012 and 2018.

At a time when we need to collaboratively act on climate change, Higashide says that riding the bus reminds us that "we're making decisions that affect each other."

About the Author

Kendra Pierre-Louis is a climate reporter focusing on the science and social impacts of climate change. She has worked for Gimlet, the New York Times *and* Popular Science. *Pierre-Louis is based in New York City.*

Access to Electric Vehicles Is an Environmental Justice Issue

By Neha Palmer

T he shift to electrified transport represents a societal and technological change on par with the industrial revolution, the New Deal and the more recent digitalization of everything. The effects will have lasting impacts on our economy and built environment. The Senate's passing of the bipartisan infrastructure bill is a historic breakthrough in the country's progress toward decarbonized transport, with $7.5 billion allocated to create charging stations across the country and another $7.5 billion to transition buses and other public transportation to zero-emission options. As we embark on the mission to increase electric vehicle (EV) adoption, it is incumbent upon all stakeholders leading the transition to ensure equitable access to the benefits.

Lack of EVs Has Disproportionate Effects

Countless studies have indicated the disproportionate impact of climate change and pollution on low-income and BIPOC communities. For example, Black Americans are 75 percent more likely than white people to live in areas near commercial facilities that produce noise, odor, traffic or emissions that directly affect the population. In the U.S., non-Hispanic white people are exposed to 17 percent less air pollution exposure than is caused by their consumption of goods and services, while Black and Hispanic people inhale 56 percent and 63 percent excess exposure, respectively, relative to their consumption. In the New York City borough of the Bronx, where median household income is $40,088 (compared to $86,553 in largely affluent Manhattan), hospitalizations for asthma are five times the national rate, a consequence of the proximity of four major highways.

EVs would undoubtedly improve health outcomes, but there are only 17 EV charging stations for the borough's 1.4 million residents.

While EVs are becoming more attainable to average consumers thanks to government incentives, battery innovation and used cars entering the market, access to charging stations is a major barrier. Installing home charging systems is expensive, and for moderate-to-low-income people living in apartments or affordable housing, it's simply not an option. Consider that nearly two thirds of renters do not have a garage or carport. Currently, most EV stations are located in higher-end shopping areas that may be difficult or inconvenient to reach for middle- to lower- income consumers, because of where they are in relation to where they live, or the types of businesses that host the stations.

Expanded Passenger Charging Is Picking Up Speed

Some cities are accelerating efforts to expand charging access. A pilot project in Kansas City. Mo., is installing EV chargers on existing street lights in residential neighborhoods that anyone can pay a fee to use. Texas utility Austin Energy has leveraged government funding for an affordability program offering unlimited access to charging ports with a $4 per month subscription. For initiatives like this to be successful in creating true equity, community engagement is essential. Organizers for the Kansas City pilot held virtual community meetings and compensated the first 100 participants for their time. They presented potential charging infrastructure locations and gathered feedback on why those sites would or would not work well for community members.

It's also important that we shift the perception of EVs as being a status symbol for eco-conscious affluent consumers. A 2017 study by the California Air Resources Board found that EV adoption increased at a faster rate in neighborhoods that saw early adoption, indicating that socioeconomic status and exposure does indeed play a role. Like with the diversity issue in tech, we need to increase representation of EV owners. A lot of this will come down to community engagement programs and automakers' marketing campaigns, with a shift in messaging that emphasizes health, environment, financial and community benefits.

What About Commercial and Public Fleets?

While much of the focus has been on passenger EVs, electrifying fleets will have a much greater impact on fighting climate change and mitigating the disproportionate effects on low-income and BIPOC communities. Thanks to corporate sustainability mandates and favorable total cost of ownership for EVs, the demand for medium to heavy-duty fleets will quickly surpass those of passenger vehicles. The large electrical demand required to power commercial electric fleets will stress an already overburdened grid. As such, on-site electricity generation, storage and demand-side management must be developed alongside charging stations to ensure cost-efficient, reliable and sustainable energy delivery. Compared to passenger EV charging, building this infrastructure will require a much more concerted effort from utilities, capital markets and the private sector. However, rapid development is critical to ensuring the benefits of electrification are distributed equally, which is currently not the case. Not only will installing charging stations along key highway corridors lower the emissions and pollutants in the areas where many low-income and BIPOC communities are situated, this will help increase access to EV charging in rural areas where fleets often have to drive through to reach their final destination.

The focus of financing and incentives historically directed to consumers needs to be extended to commercial businesses and municipalities, which are increasingly shifting public bus systems to electric. For instance, both LA Metro and New York City MTA, the two largest transit fleets in the country, plan to convert their systems to all-electric buses by 2030 and 2040, respectively.

Given how lower-income families often rely on public buses to get to their jobs, take their children to school and obtain essential services, expanding access to clean, affordable and reliable transportation is a pillar of an equitable society. And like commercial fleets, electric bus fleets come with complex energy needs that can only be met by the development of robust on-site energy and charging infrastructure.

With the emergence of energy-as-a-service providers focused on vehicle electrification, real estate developers, commercial fleet owners and municipalities now have feasible, low-risk options for deploying charging infrastructure at no upfront cost. This type of business model innovation and collaboration across sectors is what will unlock rapid electrification and equitable access.

Seizing the Opportunity for Economic Development

The technology revolution of the 1990s and early 2000s left many people behind in terms of access, employment and distribution of wealth—with ramifications the industry is still grappling with today. With the shift to electrified transport, we have the opportunity to embed equity from the start and enable a greater number of people to participate in economic development. Electrification delivers diverse employment across the value chain—including manufacturing, construction, maintenance and operations —and expands opportunities for workers in adjacent and supporting industries. Take New York, for example: a recent report projects electric transportation (ET) jobs in the state will grow 32 percent by 2024, with 882 businesses already employing 4,200 ET-related jobs in 61 counties. Thankfully, the Biden Administration is putting forth policies aimed at supporting domestic clean-energy jobs, strengthening America's EV supply chain and increasing penetration of renewables. But it's also up to utilities, the private sector, local governments and advocacy groups to ensure that we're deploying the appropriate financing models, messaging and engagement programs with equity at its core.

About the Author

Neha Palmer is CEO of TeraWatt Infrastructure, which aims to provide solutions for the large-scale electric vehicle charging infrastructure required to meet the rapid electrification of medium and heavy-duty transport and fleets.

Section 5: Feeding the Planet

Farm Protests in India Are Writing the Green Revolution's Obituary

By Aniket Aga

In September 2020, India's Narendra Modi government circumvented parliamentary procedures to push through three bills that eased restrictions on private players in agricultural markets. The move enraged farmers—especially in the northwestern state of Punjab, an epicenter of the Green Revolution since the 1950s. After protesting in vain for two months, tens of thousands of Punjab farmers began a march to New Delhi in late November. The Modi government responded by deploying paramilitary troops armed with water cannons and tear gas shells, and protected by barricades, concertina wires and deep trenches dug into freeways at the borders of the capital city.

The demonstrations have since spread across the country and represent the largest-ever mobilization of farmers in independent India. They have already claimed over 70 lives; many have died of the cold and some have committed suicide as a political statement. The standoff is not just about the repeal of the three laws, but also includes the demand that the state guarantee minimum support prices (MSPs) for all public and private purchases of produce. In a broader perspective, however, this agitation is writing the obituary of the Green Revolution.

The Green Revolution—essentially the promotion of capital-intensive industrial agriculture—was more of a Cold War stratagem than a humanitarian initiative, as recent histories have forcefully argued. After independence in 1947, peasant movements led by communists had mounted fierce pressure on the Indian National Congress, the ruling political party, to redistribute land from landlords to peasants.

But the Congress, beholden to landlords for electoral support in rural areas, was unwilling to implement comprehensive land reforms.

In this context, the U.S. government promoted the Green Revolution to preempt a Soviet-style "Red Revolution," as U.S. Agency for International Development administrator William Gaud stated in a speech in 1968. It comprised subsidized fertilizers and irrigation, rice and wheat varieties bred to absorb high fertilizer doses, and state-led training programs to assist farmers in transitioning to new practices. Given the expense, it was rolled out only in a few, well-endowed districts of Punjab and a few other states. Because bumper productions inevitably depress prices, farmers were guaranteed procurement through state-run *mandis* or market yards at MSPs declared in advance. State procurement was therefore crucial to transforming Punjab into India's breadbasket.

In sum, the Indian government held out the promise of provisioning the hungry with subsidized cereals and pumped massive investments to win over the well-off segments of landowning farmers. Alternative ideas for science-backed agricultural development, such as relying on locally available varieties and agroecological adaptations, were never seriously considered.

But as many argued, the Green Revolution package created more problems than it solved. By the 1980s, even the geographically limited package proved fiscally onerous. As state support declined, the problem of unremunerative prices and debt escalated. So did ecological crises such as falling groundwater tables, saline and degraded soils, biodiversity loss and health disorders from pesticide use—culminating in a full-blown agrarian crisis by the 1990s and an epidemic of suicides by farmers.

Modi hails the laws as watershed reforms that will usher in a new era of prosperity for farmers backed by corporate investments. On the face of it, they allow private buyers to purchase farm produce outside of the supervision of and without the payment of taxes and fees to *mandis*; limit state intervention in retail prices; and provide a framework for farming on contract to corporations.

In their details, however, the farm laws intrude upon the regulatory powers of state governments and intensify the already severe power asymmetry between corporate houses and the mass of

Indian farmers, nearly 86 percent of whom cultivate less than two hectares. Clauses like one that bars farmers—or anyone else—from seeking legal recourse over contractual disputes cement the fear that the laws stack the deck against farmers. In an incisive analysis, economist Sudha Narayanan concludes that the putative benefits for farmers have little empirical justification and, in fact, the three laws "collectively invisibilize trade area transactions, contract farming and stocking in a way that makes them unregulatable."

Farmers fear that the laws portend a total hollowing out of the state-regulated procurement at *mandis*. To this day, *mandis* signal prices with regular announcements of MSPs, and if they are weakened any further than they already have been, farmers will be fully exposed to debilitating price pressures. As Balbir Singh Rajewal, president of the Bharatiya Kisan Union (Indian Farmers' Union) explains, farmers are protesting not because the existing system is fair, but because it is being replaced with an even more inscrutable system that will further disadvantage them. The real agenda behind the laws, farmers allege, is to facilitate corporate control over agriculture and food, and Reliance and Adani Group, two of India's largest business houses, perceived to be close to the Modi government, have especially incurred the farmers' wrath.

The agitation has also garnered some support from unions of agricultural laborers, most of whom own little or no land, belong to Dalit (or oppressed) castes and come from families that have endured centuries of violence and exploitation from landed farmers, who are typically higher in the caste hierarchy. Women farmers hailing from landowning and Dalit castes are also in the forefront of the present agitation, an achievement of decades of struggle for recognition as prime movers of the agrarian economy and against caste-based sexual violence. And farmers' groups have made common cause with other protests in India, demanding that jailed political prisoners, student agitators, human rights activists and revolutionaries be released.

Underlying this broad base of discontent is the failure of the Green Revolution. Even a celebratory review in 2003 was forced to concede that the principal benefit of the package was lower food grain prices, whereas the vast majority of farmers and agricultural laborers had suffered declines in incomes. In short, the Green Revolution secured cheap cereals in exchange for justice and ecological sustainability. More recent scholarship calls for a total revision of the Green Revolution success narrative, even questioning whether there was an overall food scarcity plaguing 1950s India—the purported reason for its introduction.

In his lecture on winning the Nobel Peace Prize in 1970, Norman Borlaug, one of the "fathers" of the Green Revolution, provided an obtuse defense of the program: "Some critics have said that the green revolution has created more problems than it has solved. This I cannot accept, for I believe it is far better for mankind to be struggling with new problems caused by abundance rather than with the old problem of famine." Five decades since, we have come full circle, and it is evident that new problems of industrial agriculture have added to the old problems of hunger and malnutrition.

No amount of tinkering on the marketing end will fix a fundamentally warped and unsustainable production model, and therefore the government must concede the immediate demand to withdraw the three laws. But to actually secure a viable future for farmers, we must abandon the Green Revolution paradigm and adopt agroecological, diverse, decentralized and just agrarian and food systems.

About the Author

Aniket Aga teaches environmental studies and anthropology at Krea University in India. He is the author of Genetically Modified Democracy: Transgenic Crops in Contemporary India, *published by Yale University Press.*

Agroecology Is the Solution to World Hunger

By Raj Patel

Although it is the sharp edge of the battle to end hunger, you could be forgiven for thinking you were watching a reality TV cooking show. Under the low peak of Bwabwa Mountain in Malawi, in a village on a tributary of the Rukuru River, about 100 people gather around pots and stoves. Children crowd around a large mortar, snickering at their fathers', uncles' and neighbors' ham-fisted attempts to pound soybeans into soy milk. At another station, a village elder is being schooled by a man half his age in the virtues of sweet potato doughnuts. At yet another, a woman teaches a neighbor how he might turn sorghum into a nutritious porridge. Supervising it all, with the skill of a chef, the energy of a children's entertainer and the resolve of a sergeant, is community organizer Anita Chitaya. After helping one group with a millet sponge loaf, she moves to share a tip about how mashed soy and red beans can be turned into patties by the eager young hands of children who would typically never volunteer to eat beans.

There is an air of playful competition. Indeed, it is a competition. At the end of the afternoon the food is shared, and there are prizes for both the best-tasting food (the doughnuts win hands down) and the food most likely to be added to folks' everyday diets (the porridge triumphs because although everyone likes deep-fried food, doughnuts are a pain to cook, and the oil is very expensive).

This is a Recipe Day in Bwabwa, a village of around 800 people in northern Malawi. These festivals are sociological experiments to reduce domestic inequality and are part of a multifaceted approach to ending hunger called agroecology. Academics describe it as a science, a practice and a social movement. Agroecology applies ecology and social science to the creation and management of sustainable food systems and involves 10 or more interconnected principles, ranging from the maintenance of soil health and biodiversity to the increase of gender and intergenerational equity. More than eight million farmer groups around the world are experimenting with it and finding that compared with conventional agriculture, agroecology is able to sequester more carbon in the soil, use water more frugally, reduce dependence on external inputs by recycling nutrients such as nitrogen and phosphorus, and promote, rather than ravage, biodiversity in the soil and on farms. And on every continent, research shows that farmers who adopt agroecology have greater food security, higher incomes, better health and lower levels of indebtedness.

Chitaya told me that at the turn of the millennium, when Bwabwa's farmers were still practicing conventional agriculture, "there were times when we wouldn't be able to eat for days. My first child was malnourished." Now her oldest son, France, is a very healthy adolescent, helping teach other boys how to cook. The pediatric malnutrition clinic near Bwabwa has closed down for want of cases—though in Malawi as a whole, more than a third of the children younger than five years are stunted by malnutrition. Despite the COVID-19 pandemic, whose devastating economic effects have deepened malnutrition across the world, agroecology continues to help Bwabwa evade hunger.

Yet when policy makers attend a United Nations Food Systems Summit in the fall of 2021, the solutions on the table for world hunger will exclude agroecology. The summit's sponsors include the Gates Foundation, whose preferred solution is a set of technologies modeled on the Green Revolution. Despite a great deal of evidence that the Gates' Alliance for a Green Revolution in Africa has failed, one of its leading acolytes from Rwanda will chair the U.N. Summit. Advocates for agroecology, such as the Alliance for Food Sovereignty in Africa, which represents 200 million food producers and consumers, have too few resources to impact a process that increasingly silences their voices.

Ending hunger requires much more than pulling more food from the ground; it involves grappling with entrenched hierarchies of power. Over the past decade food production has generally outstripped demand—there is more food per person than there ever was. But because of global and regional inequalities, exacerbated by the recent pandemic, levels of hunger are higher now than in 2010. In other words, more food has accompanied more hunger. People are deprived of food not because it is scarce but because they lack the power to access it.

The global food system was originally established under colonialism, when the agriculture and land-ownership patterns of much of the tropical world were reconfigured, and tens of millions of enslaved and bonded laborers were shipped around the world to provide Europeans with cane sugar and other tropical crops for which they had developed a taste. Far from ending with colonialism, however, this system of food extraction has grown only stronger because of conditions attached to loans from international financial institutions such as the World Bank and the International Monetary Fund (IMF). To pay its debts, Africa now exports everything from roses to broth.

Agroecology frees the world's poorest farmers from such structures of control and shifts the balance of power in the global food system to people like Chitaya, one of billions who reside at the very bottom of the socioeconomic pyramid. Little wonder, then, that it is unpopular with conventional agricultural businesses, governments in the Global North and the organizers of the food systems summit. Its recognition that systemic problems require systemic solutions makes agroecology a threat.

Hunger in Malawi

Over a lifetime of trying to get to the bottom of why there is hunger and what might be done about it, I have traveled from within organizations like the U.N. and the World Bank to protest lines outside and within the World Trade Organization. During the past decade, however, I have also had a scientific education at the hands of some of the world's poorest farmers.

My first visit to Bwabwa was in 2011, at the invitation of my graduate school friend Rachel Bezner Kerr. Now a professor of development studies at Cornell University, Bezner Kerr had arrived in Malawi a decade earlier to find herself in the middle of an economic crisis. Malawi had suddenly reduced fertilizer subsidies—and that, too, while the HIV/AIDS pandemic was wreaking humanitarian and economic havoc. Farmers, most of whom practiced industrial agriculture, which requires expensive chemical inputs, were desperate. Bezner Kerr wanted to be of service as she developed a project for a master's degree, so she sought the most disadvantaged families to support in her research. She was lucky to meet Esther Lupafya, a nurse who headed the maternal and child health program at a clinic in the small town of Ekwendeni. Together they identified farmers, including Chitaya, who were ready to try a different kind of agriculture—one that would free them from dependence on global agrobusiness and its allies.

Getting to Bwabwa involves a six-hour drive north from Malawi's capital, Lilongwe. Lined with signs heralding the projects of several nongovernmental organizations and foreign aid institutions, the northern road from the Lilongwe airport tracks the eastern shore of Lake Malawi, the continent's third-largest freshwater lake. After passing northern Malawi's biggest city, Mzuzu, with its six-story Bank of Malawi Building, and the smaller town of Ekwendeni, you follow dirt roads to reach Bwabwa. Whereas the large, flat, irrigated fields off the main highway are neat monocultures of corn, the fields near the village are drier, smaller, canted at every angle and packed with twirling thickets of different crops, each tailored to the needs of the family tending it and the capacity of that particular field's ecology.

Northern Malawi did not always look like this. The first white man to visit was Scottish Presbyterian David Livingstone in 1858. His missionary campaign led to the establishment of the British Central African Protectorate, which later became Nyasaland. Photographs from the time show scrubland. British agriculturist B. E. Lilley gazed on Malawi in the 1920s and declared: "The time has not arrived when the native can be looked to as a person who can be relied upon to raise produce to anything [like] the extent that the white man raises it." Similar attitudes persist to this day, though they are now couched in contemporary language.

Keen to wring what they could from the colony's resources, the British began to export ivory and forest products, moving on to the crops that would transform Malawi's land and economy: tea, cotton, sugar and tobacco. The colonists took over the land, but they needed workers, so they imposed a hut tax, an annual household fee payable in cash. Initially families paid the colonists by selling their stores of wealth, usually livestock, until there was nothing left to liquidate. Then they sent able-bodied men to sell their labor, in Malawian plantations and the mines farther south. Debt turned self-sufficient farmers and pastoralists into manual workers, laboring for a pittance.

Debt also turned Malawi into a pawn of its creditors. Malawi became independent in 1964, only to spend the next 30 years under autocrat Hastings Banda. Western donors rewarded his iron-fisted regime with high-dollar loans to support the country's industrial development while ignoring its worsening malnutrition. Such loans became the instruments of Malawi's, and in fact Africa's, hunger. In the early postcolonial period, Africa was a net food exporter, selling 1.3 million tons a year from 1966 to 1970. But the oil-price crisis of the 1970s forced African governments to borrow even more from the World Bank and the IMF. These so-called structural adjustment loans came with strict conditions that, among other measures, slashed public spending on education and health care and privatized national assets. Further, African countries were instructed to concentrate on exports of the colonial-era crops, which would earn the dollars with which they might repay their debts.

Despite paying an average of $100 million per year to its creditors throughout the 1980s, however, Malawi remains one of the most indebted countries on Earth. Worse, devoting the richest land to growing cash crops for export, instead of food crops for subsistence, meant that structural adjustments had by the 1990s turned Africa into an importer of a quarter of its food. Between

120

2016 and 2018 Africa imported 85 percent of its food from outside the continent—a debilitating dependence.

Trial, Review, Exchange

In 1992 a national survey revealed that 55 percent of Malawian children had failed to reach the appropriate height for their age—a key measure of malnutrition. The government tried to defy the austerity imposed by international banks and donors by subsidizing fertilizers for farmers but eventually caved to their demands to instead prioritize paying off the loans. Lupafya and Bezner Kerr began their work soon after these supports were removed, establishing the Soils, Food and Healthy Communities (SFHC) initiative in Ekwendeni in 2000. Starting with 30 farmers, the SFHC now works with more than 6,000 people across 200 villages to promote agroecology.

Along with Chitaya and others, the women began with a round of experiments, intercropping local groundnuts and other legumes. This double-legume system allowed the farmers to harvest nuts and beans for their children and then dig the nitrogen-rich residue back into the soil to boost maize production—without buying fertilizer. Some farmers went further, experimenting with vegetable intercropping patterns. Simultaneously, the SFHC developed a system of peer review, in which the participants met regularly to discuss measures to improve soil fertility. Women farmers had long been exchanging seeds and knowledge to grow finger millet, a drought-tolerant plant that produces highly nutritious grains that make for hearty porridge and, if you can stomach it, sour beer. The SFHC formalized this tradition of evaluating and sharing information.

By running trials of different legume cropping systems in a "mother" location in the middle of different villages, farmers could then adopt "baby" trials in their own fields based on their preferences for soil health, nutrition and the time they could spare to tend the crops. Through discussions and iterations over the years, initial trials grew from a few dozen households to reach thousands of farmers, with a pigeon-pea-and-groundnut combination proving to be the most successful in fixing nitrogen. As the soil improved, some farmers, many of them women, did well enough not only to feed their families but also to sell a respectable surplus at the local market.

Still, every farmer, every field and every season are different, so the experiments continued. Some women tried seemingly incongruous combinations such as soy and tomatoes—originating in Asia and the Americas, respectively—alongside indigenous African varieties such as finger millet. (Millet cultivation had earlier been discouraged because the grain could not be exported for dollars, but it persisted because women often brew it into beer as a means of earning extra income.) In Bwabwa, the fields are a mixture of foreign and native varieties, selected through trial and observation, with networks of farmers exchanging knowledge and ideas and reviewing one another's work.

That openness to experimentation and adaptation explains why, around March, it is possible to see in the unpromising red soil a cultivation system that looks like it may not belong. Tall rows of corn burst from the ground. Twirling around them are pole beans, and at their feet are the fat, dark fan-shaped leaves of local pumpkin, together with their blossoms. In Mesoamerican agriculture, this kind of technique is known as the three sisters: corn, beans and squash.

In Malawi, locally adapted varieties work together in similar ways: the corn or millet provides the starchy cereal that forms the backbone of every meal. The stalks also scaffold the beans, which yield protein and fix nitrogen. Root nodules in legumes (such as beans and groundnuts) are a site of symbiosis between the plant and rhizobia bacteria. The plant provides the bacteria with energy; the bacteria take nonreactive nitrogen molecules from the air and turn them into ammonia and amino acids for the host. This works well for cereals, which need bioavailable nitrogen to do well. The pumpkin (or other squash) provides big leaves for shading out weeds, and its flowers attract beneficial insects that keep pest pressure down. Plus, at the end of the season, there are gourds.

When put together, these crops produce more food per unit area than when they grow alone. Polycultures are demonstrably more abundant than monocultures. After harvest, the crop residue is reincorporated into the soil to build fertility and structure for the soil's biome.

In the early 2000s, as soil fertility in Bwabwa improved, some of the poorest women began to harvest an abundance of cereal, beans and vegetables. Interest in the cropping techniques spread. But despite real improvements in food production, child malnutrition remained puzzlingly high. Some of the farmers in the project, excited that they were becoming agronomists, started to wonder how to tackle the problem more directly. As they would discover, they had made progress in freeing themselves from external structures of power—but had yet to tackle internal ones.

Wrestling Down Patriarchy

Through her work at the pediatric clinic, Lupafya had formed a suspicion: tradition was partly to blame for infant malnutrition. Ethnographic research across the SFHC villages confirmed her hunch. Within the patriarchal extended family, mothers-in-law have authority over their daughters-in-law. When an ill-founded parenting tip—that children cry because they are not being given solid food—is propagated through these networks, young mothers often find themselves counseled to wean their children at the age of two months. This advice runs counter to overwhelming scientific evidence that exclusive breastfeeding for six months and then a mix of breast and solid food until two years of age offer children the best start in life.

Lupafya crafted a way to walk the tightrope of respectful disagreement. The SFHC trained village women and men as facilitators to broker difficult conversations, particularly those between mothers- and daughters-in-law. Through monthly meetings and leadership from Lupafya and others, the science spread, and the misinformation was dispelled.

Lupafya learned something as well. "Change begins with denial," she told me. "It is the one who debates the most who will change." Having tackled the availability of food and breastfeeding practices, the grassroots social scientists moved to another determinant of infant malnutrition they had identified: domestic violence and, more broadly, patriarchy. Women's autonomy is linked with improved child nutrition indicators. As they observed, gender inequality meant that mothers had to spend time cooking, cleaning, managing the farm and breastfeeding. To have men help in domestic labor would increase women's autonomy. The question was: How do you get men to cook?

To find out how this transformative change happened, I worked with the SFHC team for more than a decade, documenting Chitaya's work in a film called *The Ants & the Grasshopper*. Chitaya had first met Lupafya when she visited the pediatric nutrition clinic. The older woman, Mama Lupafya as she is called, had supported her in a difficult marriage, one into which Chitaya had been coerced. Through attending workshops hosted by the SFHC, then by finding work as one of its trainers, and through long and difficult work in her home, Chitaya has transformed her marriage into one characterized by equality.

There are times when her husband, Christopher Nyoni, struggles to pull his weight in the house. He is afflicted by night blindness, a possible consequence of his own malnutrition early in life. When it gets dark, he is no longer able to cook or clean and needs help finding his way around the house. But by the light of day, he can be seen hunched over a stove or doing laundry or fetching water—all of which are traditionally women's work. It is a sign of Chitaya's success that Nyoni is keen to break with patriarchal tradition: "I do not want my son to get married the way I did," he told me.

The pathway to transforming this and other gender relationships in Bwabwa lay through changing the culture around food. An initial effort to achieve this shift involved door-to-door organizing. Members of the SFHC would visit households with an expert and offer to teach men how to cook novel foods, such as soy. After an enthusiastic afternoon gathered around a stove, surrounded by exhortations to do better, the men promised they would change. They did not. So the SFHC farmers brainstormed an alternative.

A constant worry for men was the social stigma of doing the effeminate work of cooking. "What if my friends see me?" asked Winston Zgambo. Having tried to cater to men's embarrassment by offering private cooking lessons, the SFHC team tried the opposite. They held public cooking competitions for whole families. On Recipe Days, all men were involved in cooking—and it was fun. By gamifying the change in behavior through offering prizes and social recognition for success, the women cracked open the possibilities for changing not just food culture, but inequalities in power within the home.

Data from the SFHC's work speak for themselves. Participation in the program moved children from being below the average weight for their age to surpassing the average. A recent study in which women farmers showed other mothers how to farm led to a range of benefits, from increased dietary diversity for children to lower maternal depression rates and higher rates of fathers' participation in chores.

A Teeming Future

Agroecology means taking care not just of all humans but also of the ecosystems on which we depend. Under chemical agriculture, farmers grow a single crop. They buy fertilizers, pesticides, herbicides and access to water, and if necessary, they rent pollinators to maximize the yield. They use the revenue from selling the harvest to pay their bills and debts. In agroecology, farmers find ways not to exterminate pests but to reach an ecological equilibrium. They accept a little crop loss while providing habitats for predators and introducing other forms of biological control to obtain a much more robust and resilient ecosystem. In northern Malawi, biodiversity is part of the SFHC's success, as it is in every successful agroecological system. There are more insects, amphibians, reptiles, fish, birds and mammals in these landscapes than in the barren green deserts of modern monoculture.

In a world of extreme weather, agroecological diversity—both social and biological—is a source of resilience. When Hurricane Ike ploughed through Cuba in September 2008, it left trees and debris littering the fields. In Sancti Spíritus province, researchers noticed that the farms that followed the principles of conventional agriculture, with vast expanses of the same kind of crop, took around six months to recover from the devastation. But the most diversified farms, with tall plantains, fruit trees, perennial crops and ground cover, were able to recover 80 percent of their prestorm capacity in just two months. With high canopy trees blown over, more light fell on other plants in the understory, which grew faster: the diversity constituted a kind of botanical insurance portfolio. Moreover, families living on diversified farms could save some trees the morning after the storm, when conventional farm workers were far from the fields where their labor was seasonally contracted.

Agroecology also enables income resilience. Small farmers typically receive very little support. Instead they need to manage the flows of cash around the farm themselves. Conventional agriculture has one big burst of cash at harvest time, which may or may not be enough to pay off farming-related debts and dwindles throughout the year. With agroecology, on the other hand, income streams can be augmented by means of crops that mature in the leanest times. In Mexico, for instance, one group of farmers supplements its corn income with countercyclical honey and coffee harvests.

In the absence of reliable banks, farmers have sometimes turned to creating their own circular economies and exchanges. Many places have local grain stores that help to manage the booms and busts in harvests and hunger. In Bwabwa a few years ago women set up a credit circle to help manage cash flow and to develop other income streams, such as the sale of "climate change stoves," cooking stands that require much less wood than conventional wood-burning methods. A dozen women pooled their resources and took turns borrowing the cash and then repaying it. But the savings circle was wiped out in the IMF-mandated devaluation of the Malawian kwacha (currency) in 2012.

The COVID-19 crisis has made farmers' lives harder. Rising food prices have strained finances, and with resources diverted to emergency mitigation measures so that communities could stay home and stay safe, everyone's life has become harder. Yet agroecological practices appear to have enabled the SFHC's villages to endure the pandemic better than communities outside the project.

Feed the World

What happens in Malawi and among the hundreds of millions of farmers experimenting with new kinds of agroecology matters for the planet. Agroecology offers the ability to do what governments, corporations and aid agencies have failed to do: end hunger. For a while, it might have been easy to respond to agroecology by saying "that's all very nice, but it won't feed the world." But farming families that engage in agroecology have improved indicators of income and nutrition. From Nepal to the Netherlands, when agroecology is not confined to the field but extends into the home with equality and into community networks of exchange and care, farmers are financially and physically better off.

With ideas from the World Economic Forum and with support from the food and chemicals industry, the solutions on the table at the U.N. meeting are far less imaginative. Nor do they go far enough to remedy or even acknowledge the environmental and other harms committed by industrial agriculture. This supposedly scientific method of growing food is one of the largest drivers of climate change. Algae blooms from nitrogen and phosphate pollution are devastating aquatic life. Pristine forests are falling to ranches and plantations. Aquifers are being drained for thirsty cash crops. Fertile soil is turning to sterile dust as synthetic chemicals kill essential microbes, and pesticides are decimating insects on which extended chains of life depend.

This past July the Rockefeller Foundation reported that whereas Americans spent $1.1 trillion on food in 2019, the additional external health, environmental, climate change, biodiversity and economic costs associated with the food industry were $2.1 trillion. That is quite a debt—and one that the industry will never have to pay. The rest of the world shoulders the cost. Yet the firms behind this damage are the ones offering solutions at the summit.

We know how to do better. Agroecology more than fits the bill—not only because the crops grown are more diverse but because the social arrangements that surround them are more cognizant of power. Industrial agriculture's hidden costs are precisely the ones agroecology makes explicit. Its pathways reward the acumen of those on the front lines, support the livelihoods of the poor and protect the biodiversity of the planet. Its researchers and practitioners are already hard at work, teaching and learning from one another.

Such networks of knowledge undo the colonial savior complexes to which many development experts are still tied. Instead, under agroecology, as Chitaya puts it, "women can teach men, Black people can teach white people, the poor can teach the rich." She reflects on the certainties of struggle ahead, particularly as the powerful seem to be doubling down on industrial agriculture. "So much has been lost. But it's never too late to change."

About the Author

Raj Patel is a professor of public affairs at the University of Texas at Austin and a member of the International Panel of Experts on Sustainable Food Systems. His books include Stuffed and Starved *and* The Value of Nothing. *Most recently, he co-directed with Zak Piper the award-winning documentary* The Ants & the Grasshopper.

Designer Crops of the Future Must Be Better Tailored for Women in Agriculture

By Vivian Polar and Matty Demont

For all the progress that scientists have made in breeding crops that feed more people, these breakthroughs typically elude a core demographic in low-income countries that rely on agriculture: women.

Advances in seed genetics are estimated to be responsible for up to 60 percent of yield increases in farmers' fields in recent years by making crops hardier and faster-maturing. However, only a third of crops grown by sub-Saharan African farmers in 2010 were the latest varieties of genetically improved plants; the uptake is as low as 5 percent for women-led households in that region. In some cases, modern varieties may be more difficult for women to harvest, process or cook but ultimately, scientists need more research to fully understand the traits that make crops desirable and viable for women as well as men

Women make up more than 40 percent of the global agricultural workforce, and an even greater proportion in developing countries. In order to improve global food security and end hunger, crop breeders need better market intelligence to understand the qualities women prefer in crops so they, too, can access the gains from genetically engineered crops.

Whereas men who farm are more likely to prioritize high yields and disease resistance, since this typically equates to higher incomes upon selling, women who farm often prioritize other needs in their roles as mothers, caregivers and custodians of households. The implication for crop breeders is that for a new variety to be widely adopted by both men and women, it must be attractive both to men looking to increase earnings, and women, who take on a greater responsibility for household nutrition.

129

Scientists are starting to make headway in understanding the needs of women farmers. For instance, in a forthcoming study by the International Potato Center (CIP), researchers working on new varieties of sweet potato for East Africa found that 80 percent of stakeholders were aware that women prioritised the taste of sweet potato varieties over all other traits because this impacts the likelihood of their children eating it. Another example is demand for rice fragrance in South and Southeast Asia, which was found to be mainly driven by women.

This is reinforced by other studies that indicate that the ease of cooking for staple crops such as cassava is also a key factor that influences the uptake of new varieties among women. They tend to prefer varieties that cook quickly during boiling, which is determined by factors such as age, phytic acid levels and larger starch granules.

But as well as women's preferences, crop breeders also need more market intelligence to better understand the challenges and barriers to uptake that women face and their role in household decision-making on what crop varieties to grow. For example, research shows that women are more likely to take on the time-consuming manual work of weeding, threshing and cooking; weeding a single hectare of sorghum by hand takes up to 324 hours of labor. In East Africa, maize adoption lagged because women objected to higher-yield varieties of hard dent maize that were difficult to grind and so increased their workload. Women are more likely to use traits that reduce the drudgery of agriculture for them.

Early efforts to factor in these considerations in the crop breeding process have included the development of G+ Tools by CGIAR (formerly the Consultative Group on International Agricultural Research), the organization for which we work. It's the world's largest publicly funded agricultural organization. This tool kit provides a framework to support targeting specific segments of the population to determine the potential implications of traits or varieties for gender equality. The tools include questions about how a new product might increase drudgery, displace other forms of income or rely too heavily on inputs such as irrigation, mechanization or fertilizer, which may be out of reach for women.

The tools, which unite the expertise of social scientists, gender experts and breeders, have been piloted in Uganda, Nigeria and Zimbabwe to set priorities for the development of new lines of sweet potato, cassava and beans. In Nigeria, this has led to the cassava breeding program prioritizing traits that are important to women who process cassava-based foods, including sweetness, low fiber, low moisture levels, ease of peeling and the preferred color for consumers.

Breeders also need to go beyond the field to understand the needs of women in agribusiness at every stage of the value chain. With more investment into projects and initiatives that subsidize the rollout of new varieties, farmers and processors could afford to test them and see their benefits before adopting them in full, so as not to compromise their traditional sources of income and food.

And for all the crops that provide better yields for smallholders, those that perish quickly or that need specific storage conditions to reach market or specialist equipment to process will be less profitable and therefore less likely to be adopted.

Among the existing innovations that hold promise for better nutrition and livelihoods against the pressures of climate change are vitamin-enriched sweet potato and cassava, iron and zinc-biofortified and low glycemic index rice, high-yielding maize and fast-cooking beans. But fine-tuning these varieties to maximize their uptake among men and women needs more research into their needs on the ground.

An estimated $39 million investment is needed over the next three years to design these crops and tailor them, but the return is likely to translate to higher incomes, improved food security and greater levels of equality for up to 125 million farmers, small businesses, and consumers across Africa and South Asia alone by 2030. And by meeting the needs of all farmers, improved varieties can future-proof food systems for everyone.

This is an opinion and analysis article, and the views expressed by the author or authors are not necessarily those of Scientific American.

About the Authors

Vivian Polar is the gender and innovation senior specialist at the CGIAR International Potato Center (CIP) CGIAR (formerly the Consultative Group on International Agricultural Research).

Matty Demont is the research leader, markets, consumers and nutrition, at the CGIAR International Rice Research Institute (IRRI) of CGIAR (formerly the Consultative Group on International Agricultural Research).

The Future of Fish Farming May Be Indoors

By Laura Poppick

On a projection screen in front of a packed room in a coastal Maine town, computer-animated salmon swim energetically through a massive oval tank. A narrator's voice soothingly points out water currents that promote fish exercise and ideal meat texture, along with vertical mesh screens that "optimize fish densities and tank volume." The screens also make dead fish easy to remove, the narrator cheerily adds.

The video is part of a pitch made in 2018 for an ambitious $500-million salmon farm that Norway-based firm, Nordic Aquafarms, plans to build in Belfast, Maine, complete with what Nordic says will be among the world's largest aquaculture tanks. It is one of a handful of projects in the works by companies hoping these highly mechanized systems will change the face fish farming—by moving it indoors.

If it catches on, indoor aquaculture could play a critical role in meeting the needs of a swelling human population, Nordic CEO Erik Heim says. He believes it could do so without the pollution and other potential threats to wild fish that can accompany traditional aquaculture—although the indoor approach does face environmental challenges of its own. "There's always some risk, but the risk of the land-based system is a small percentage of the risk of an outdoor system," says Michael Timmons, an environmental engineer at Cornell University who has studied aquaculture for more than 20 years and is not involved in the Nordic project.

Fish farming has often been touted as an extremely efficient way to produce animal protein: the Global Aquaculture Alliance claims 100 kilograms of fish feed can deliver up to 15 times more meat than an equivalent amount fed to cows. The industry has gained international traction, with farmed fish surpassing wild-caught ones in the global food supply in 2014. But traditional fish-farming methods come with significant environmental drawbacks. For example, salmon farmers in Norway and Chile—the world leaders in salmon production—typically use open-ocean cages that corral fish in suspended netting or pens. This setup allows waste to flow directly into the environment, along with pathogens and parasites that can infect wild populations. Open-air pond farms—found worldwide and representing the most common type of aquaculture in China, the top global producer of farmed fish—also have a track record of polluting local waterways with fish effluent and veterinary medicines that are used to keep disease at bay.

Timmons contends land-based indoor systems can greatly reduce such risks. They isolate fish from the environment and remove most of the waste from the water using recirculating aquaculture systems (RAS), which are akin to filtration systems in a household fish aquarium, he says. But to date, indoor RAS farms have made up only a tiny fraction of the global market and are much smaller than Nordic's planned operation. For example, Blue Ridge Aquaculture—the world's largest RAS tilapia farm, located in Virginia—produces less than 10 percent of the quantity of fish Nordic expects to produce in Maine.

This recirculating technology has existed in some form since the 1970s, but has evolved enough in recent years that the Monterey Bay Aquarium's Seafood Watch now ranks RAS-farmed fish as one of the most sustainable seafood choices available. So "the natural thing to do is to scale up," Heim told Maine residents during his recent presentation. The Belfast operation would include 18 of what Heim says would be among the world's largest aquaculture tanks—each three times the volume of an Olympic pool—and would ultimately produce 33,000 tons of fish, or roughly 8 percent of U.S. consumption, each year. The company plans to construct a similar farm in Norway next year that would contain tanks the same size, he says.

Although there are questions as to whether scaling up increases such a system's environmental riskiness, some experts think the technology can make a sustainable transition to the big time. Community members in Heim's audience voiced concerns about how wastewater might affect nearby coastal waters, but Timmons says the small amount of water discharged from RAS systems (from tank overflow and spray-cleaning waste from filters) is often cleaner than when it enters. Water in RAS tanks flows through a bubbling container called a bio-filter, in which bacteria consume fish urine and convert it into a form of nitrogen that is safe for the fish and environment, says Michael Schwarz, director of the Virginia Seafood Agricultural Research and Extension Center. Physical filters gather fish feces and leftover food that can be stored away and resold as compost or raw material for biogas. Ozone treatment helps break down frothy organic solids, and ultraviolet light is used to kill pathogens.

This technology has already been tested and automated enough that scaling up can be as straightforward as "doubling the batter" for a batch of cookies, says Schwarz, who is not involved in the Belfast project. "There shouldn't be any surprise if you design it properly and operate it properly," he says. "If there is a surprise, someone didn't do their job."

This risk of human error should not be overlooked, says Brian Peterson, director of the National Cold Water Marine Aquaculture Center in Maine, where he uses recirculating systems to raise salmon for research purposes. Bio-security routines that require sanitizing hands and dipping shoes in disinfectant bins minimize the risk of disease and the need for antibiotics that other forms of aquaculture heavily rely on, says Peterson, who has advised Nordic Aquafarms regarding best practices. However, just one employee who fails to complete the process correctly or neglects other basic protocol could contaminate the operation—with pathogens potentially looping through the recirculating system and killing an entire tank of fish. Large-scale companies could guard against this with monitoring equipment that lets them respond quickly to any issues, Peterson says, adding that strict government permits require routine monitoring that would also detect unusual levels of discharge in wastewater.

The real environmental toll of big indoor systems will depend on the capacity of local infrastructure, including the water supply, Timmons says. Recirculating systems can recycle more than 90 percent of tank water but some of it does get lost to evaporation or absorbed in solid waste each day. He calculates that a farm the size of the Belfast facility would (after the initial tank fill) consume about 1.65 billion liters of freshwater per year—roughly equivalent to the water use of about 12,000 people. But he notes even in a town of fewer than 7,000 people, like Belfast, this is within the capacity of the local aquifer—and is dwarfed by the volume of water the farm would recycle each year. In more drought-prone regions indoor aquaculture facilities could release wastewater for irrigating agricultural fields, reducing the water burden, Timmons adds.

Pending state and federal permitting the Belfast facility will break ground in 2019, and Timmons believes it could pave the way for similar systems around the world. "If this facility is as successful as it appears it can be," he says, "then that will certainly incentivize others to do similar types of farms."

Robotic Bees Could Support Vertical Farms Today and Astronauts Tomorrow

By Molly Glick

I n vertical farming operations, artificial lights and artificial intelligence coax plants, stacked densely on towering shelves rather than spread over a field, to grow indoors with minimal human intervention. That's the goal. But despite lofty promises of bringing fresh produce to local markets, these systems have not yet provided a climate-friendly way to feed the world's growing population. Can robotic "bees," a buzzy technology straight out of science fiction, rescue these high-tech operations?

The world's first commercial vertical farm opened in Singapore in 2012. More businesses cropped up in the following years, with major players such as Infarm and AeroFarms securing hundreds of millions in funding over the next decade. With the help of sustainable systems such as hydroponics, as well as artificial intelligence to closely monitor plant growth and water usage, some companies and experts claim these futuristic farms could tackle global food insecurity—without the massive land and water footprint of conventional operations.

These farms "have the potential to contribute a meaningful amount to our diets," says Thomas Graham, who researches controlled environment agriculture at the University of Guelph in Ontario. And companies can place them nearly anywhere.

Many vertical farms' hopes have dried up over the past year, however. Recent inflation and worldwide skyrocketing energy prices, fueled by Russia's invasion of Ukraine, rendered these farms' near-constant electricity demand unaffordable. This past fall Infarm announced it was laying off more than half of its employees, and AeroFarms recently filed for bankruptcy. Meanwhile other vertical farm ventures are also facing financial challenges.

It doesn't help that vertical farms currently have a limited range of offerings; most grow only greens such as lettuce and herbs because they use low amounts of water and are relatively easy to cultivate indoors via hydroponics thanks to their speedy development. "Some of the work we're doing is moving past just leafy greens," Graham says. "You can't feed the world on lettuce."

To truly take on food insecurity, vertical farms must expand their offerings, and that means finding a way to bring pollinators into high-tech indoor farming operations. Around one third of the crops we eat require pollinators such as bees and bats to grow. It's difficult to get the job done in a vertical farm because domesticated honeybees, one of the most popular pollinators for commercial growers, have trouble navigating under artificial light, and pollinating by hand is extremely time intensive and thus expensive. To solve the problem, researchers have been working on robotic pollinators for more than a decade. But such pollinators have only recently made their way to universities and commercial operations.

Bee Bots to the Rescue

Bots aren't new to farms. Since the mid-20th century researchers have explored ways to automate agriculture, including tractors with automated steering. By the 1980s and 1990s, engineers had begun tinkering with task-specific devices such as a robotic melon harvester and tomato-picking robots. Companies are now developing autonomous bots to harvest a variety of produce, and some devices can also accomplish additional tasks, including weeding, pesticide spraying and disease monitoring. Artificial intelligence helps most of these tools organize and process information from their onboard sensors—often multispectral cameras, which can pick up on differences in the types of light reflected by plants. Those differences provide clues about a crop's health, such as ripeness in fruit or signs of damage.

Although most agricultural-machine research still focuses on produce-picking bots, more teams are now aiming to automate pollination as well, says Mahla Nejati, a research fellow at the

University of Auckland in New Zealand, who works on farming-oriented robotics and AI systems. For her Ph.D. project, Nejati developed the computer vision system for an autonomous kiwi- and apple-picking bot designed for orchards. Eventually, her colleagues had a revelation: because they were already picking robotically, it would have been "better to have started earlier with the pollination," Nejati says.

Now scientists and businesses around the world are grappling with the best ways to design and implement robo pollinators. This is not a simple task, says Yu Gu, a roboticist at West Virginia University, who is developing a six-armed pollinating machine called the StickBug. To build widely useable pollinators, "I think it's a big problem that there's so many types of flowers and so many types of agriculture settings," he says.

Some researchers have carried their work outside of academia and into the market. Siddharth Jadhav, who previously studied drone aerodynamics at the National University of Singapore, founded a company called Polybee in 2019. He and his colleagues adapt widely available mini drones for various types of indoor agriculture operations, including vertical farms and greenhouses. Polybee's AI-powered software instructs drones equipped with color camera sensors that measure key traits for growers to fly near plants. Then the drones carefully disturb the air around them to vibrate flowers when the conditions inside greenhouses (such as temperature and humidity) are optimal for pollination, Jadhav says. This activity shakes the pollen out of the flower and kicks off the fertilization process.

Polybee currently sells its pollination system to commercial tomato greenhouses in Australia. (Compared with many other food crops, tomato pollination is relatively straightforward because the plants' flowers have both male and female parts.) The team has also run trials with indoor vertical farming companies, Jadhav says, although "we do not have many commercial vertical farms that grow fruit crops at scale yet."

An Israel-based company called Arugga also sells bots to tomato greenhouses. Its roving ground robot, aptly named Polly, moves between rows of plants and blasts pulses of air to prompt pollination. The process is mostly autonomous. For now, however, human operators must move Polly between rows by operating a tablet. Arugga may eventually delve into vertical farming but only if that market becomes more profitable, says Eytan Heller, the company's co-founder and vice president of business development.

Still, if robotic pollinators do pan out for vertical farms, they could offer multiple advantages. For one, they could reduce infections between plants because bees can spread diseases that cause major damage to farms. For more than two decades, scientists around the world have suggested that bumblebees can spread viruses to previously uninfected tomatoes that can render them unsellable. Commercially developed bees deployed in greenhouses can also slip outside and infect wild bees nearby, which are already experiencing a rapid decline that is largely linked to factors such as climate change, urbanization and pesticide use. This is especially damaging for the plants that rely on those outdoor pollinators because they can't fall back on their own mechanical substitutes. According to Nejati, bots perform best indoors, where they can move around highly structured environments and avoid unpredictable weather and temperatures.

What's Next for Robo Bees?

While Polybee and Arugga claim they've got the tomato pollination game down pat, they're still working on modifying their products to work with other types of plants. Polybee is currently running trials with strawberries, and Arugga says its tools can be adjusted to work with plenty of other crops, such as strawberries and blueberries.

But each plant comes with its own complexities, Gu says. While Arugga plans to use its pulsing-air method for various types of fruit, Gu and his colleagues have found that certain varieties may require direct contact with robots, similar to the natural method performed by bees. After collaborating with a range of experts, including entomologists and horticulturalists, he thinks that some types of berries, for example, likely benefit from contact-based pollination. Graham agrees that certain berries probably would benefit from direct interactions with robots, perhaps small drones.

Regardless of the fruit, bots will have to work gently to avoid damaging flowers, which tend to be delicate. Gu compares the pollination process to "robotic surgery" and says that, for now, the drone airflow method will likely be limited to working with several plants at once rather than individuals. "The crop that needs precision pollination [is] disturbed by the airflow," he says. "It's difficult to operate that precisely."

Even if robotic pollinators rescue vertical farms from obsolescence, it's unlikely that any type of indoor agriculture can entirely replace the fields humans have relied on for millennia. But he suggests that vertical farms could supplement outdoor crops without taking up too much space. For instance, they can be built on abandoned pieces of land. "This is a complementary way of doing things," Graham says. "We need to rethink agriculture in the face of climate change and population growth, but [vertical farms] shouldn't be looked at as competitive—because they're not."

Vertical farms could additionally aid another location that's short on natural resources: outer space. Graham, who also researches food production on the final frontier, says robotic pollinators could be particularly helpful in this environment. While scientists already plan to bring living insects to space to work as pollinators and to eat waste, the insects' metal counterparts would likely live longer. ("Worker" bumblebees only survive for a few weeks.) Astronauts could even 3-D-print these tools off-planet.

"Space is a neat field because nothing is really off the table," he says. "It's all under consideration, and ultimately—like most things— [space farming will] probably be some sort of hybrid."

About the Author

Molly Glick is a freelance science journalist based in New York City. Their writing has appeared in Inverse, Discover, Popular Science *and other publications. You can follow them on X (formerly Twitter) @mollyglick and read more of their work on their website.*

Lab-Grown Meat Approved for Sale: What You Need to Know

By Joanna Thompson

At long last, a sandwich made with lab-grown chicken may be on the menu—at least if you live in the U.S. In June 2023, the U.S. Department of Agriculture granted its first-ever approval of cell-cultured meat produced by two companies, GOOD Meat and UPSIDE Foods. Both grow small amounts of chicken cells into slabs of meat—no slaughter required. It was the final regulatory thumbs-up that the California-based companies needed in order to sell and serve their products in the U.S.

The approval comes less than a year after the Food and Drug Administration declared the companies' products safe to eat, and it represents a major milestone for the burgeoning cultured meat industry. But it doesn't mean lab-grown steaks will be hitting supermarket shelves tomorrow. For now, both companies have been given the go-ahead to sell strictly chicken products at a select handful of restaurants. They'll need additional approval to market cell-cultivated beef, pork or seafood.

Around 90 percent of the U.S. population eats meat regularly. But a growing number of Americans harbor concerns about the current meat industry's environmental impact, which accounts for about 14.5 percent of global carbon emissions. Massive livestock operations can also be breeding grounds for harmful antibiotic-resistant bacteria. What's more, they generate tons of waste and can pollute local waterways with nutrient runoff from manure. And the animals themselves often live relatively short lives, confined to cramped cages and standing in their own filth. "We think the current way of producing meat is at the very tip of the spear of all these harms," says GOOD Meat CEO Josh Tetrick.

Still, people are drawn to eating meat for a variety of reasons, such as cultural significance and tradition or its nutritional value as a protein source—not to mention its taste. Cultured meat companies, which bill themselves as sustainable and cruelty-free, hope their products will offer a way for meat lovers to enjoy a juicy burger or fried chicken with a clean conscience. "I put myself in that category," says Amy Chen, COO of UPSIDE Foods. "We call ourselves 'conflicted carnivores.'"

A lab-grown chicken nugget starts the classic way: with an egg. Food scientists sample stem cells from a fertilized chicken egg and then test the cells for resilience, taste, and the ability to divide and create more cells. Next the scientists can freeze the best cell lines for future use.

When it's time to start production, food scientists submerge the cells in a stainless steel vat of nutrient-rich broth containing all the ingredients cells need to grow and divide. After a few weeks, the cells begin to adhere to one another and produce enough protein to harvest. Finally, the scientists texturize the meat by mixing, heating or shearing it—GOOD Meat uses an extruder—and press it into nugget or cutlet shape.

The overall production process is relatively simple, says Vítor Santo, GOOD Meat's cell agriculture director. "The biggest challenge right now is definitely building the manufacturing capacity," he says. UPSIDE Foods' COO, Amy Chen, concurs. "Industrial farming has had a head start," she says. But now that both companies have USDA and FDA approval, they can start to build up the infrastructure to cultivate enough meat to ship products across the U.S.

For now, their cultured chicken will only be available in a couple of restaurants. Bar Crenn, a Michelin-starred restaurant in San Francisco, will serve UPSIDE Foods. And celebrity chef José Andrés, a member of GOOD Meat's board of directors, will serve the company's cultured chicken at one of his restaurants in Washington, D.C.

Until cultured meat is produced on a larger scale, its proposed environmental benefits remain untested. "The presumption—and I say 'presumption' carefully—is that, yes, you'll have a more sustainable food production system," says David Kaplan, a bioengineer at Tufts

University. Cultured meat production facilities, at the very least, will consume drastically less land and water than traditional agriculture and directly emit fewer greenhouse gases, though their total eventual carbon footprint at a mass-production scale is unclear.

Sustainability plus flavor is a promise that plant-based protein companies, such as the meatless juggernaut Impossible Foods, have been trying to deliver for nearly a decade. While these products have gained popularity—and landed on fast-food menus—they haven't seen the level of adoption the industry had been hoping for. Cell-cultivated meats could help bridge that gap. "Ultimately, we think people will be more likely to switch if the product is actually meat," Tetrick explains.

If cultured meat is both slaughter-free and better for the environment, will any vegetarians adopt it into their diet? "We have a range of views," says Richard McIlwain, chief executive of the Vegetarian Society of the United Kingdom. Some vegetarians are stoked about the prospect of cell-cultivated meat, but about half would prefer to avoid it, according to one poll. Acceptance is a little higher for the rest of the public: nearly two thirds of U.S. citizens are at least willing to give lab-grown meat a try.

For folks who keep a kosher or halal diet, the issue is a bit less clear-cut. In 2021 Indonesian Islamic authorities ruled that cultivated meat was not halal, though other Muslim leaders are open to the possibility of halal certification depending on how the cell lines are harvested. A cell cultivation start-up based in Israel is currently seeking market approval for its kosher-certified meat.

When the products do hit supermarket shelves, Chen says, "they will actually bear the stamp and seal that you expect on a piece of meat": a little round tag certifying USDA inspection. The labels will also include the prefix "cell-cultured" to distinguish the meat from conventional barnyard fare. And they will lack an official "vegetarian" stamp of approval. The Vegetarian Society's standpoint is that lab-grown meat doesn't qualify as vegetarian or vegan because it contains cells originally sampled from an animal. The organization, however, will consider creating a new label to certify it as "cruelty-free" or "slaughter-free," McIlwain says.

"I think it's going to need its own criteria," he adds. "But we are very excited about [cell-cultivated meat] from a societal perspective."

About the Author

Joanna Thompson s an insect enthusiast and former Scientific American *intern. She is based in New York City. Follow Thompson on X (formerly Twitter) @ jojofoshosho0.*

This Shrub Could Supply Rubber, Insect Repellent and Glue

By Ula Chrobak

The sage-green, waist-high shrub guayule might look like just one of the many scraggly bushes that dot the hills and valleys of the Chihuahuan Desert in Mexico and the southwestern U.S. But its nondescript stalks and leaves harbor a panoply of botanical treasures, including rubber that Indigenous people used hundreds of years ago to make balls for games.

For decades, researchers have been investigating guayule (*Parthenium argentatum*) as a potential commercial source of natural rubber. The market is currently dominated by rubber sourced from *Hevea brasiliensis* trees in Southeast Asia, and it's hard for guayule in the U.S. to compete with those large operations, which have lower labor costs. Farmers in the Southwest tend to favor more lucrative crops, such as alfalfa and cotton.

But two converging developments may be about to change guayule's prospects. Fungal infestations of monocultured *Hevea* trees have caused steep drops in global natural rubber supplies in recent years. Meanwhile the Southwest's worst drought in more than a millennium has reduced the water available to farmers, making it harder to grow alfalfa, cotton and other thirsty crops. Guayule, on the other hand, is drought-tolerant. And it can be grown and harvested for several years without tilling the soil. That undisturbed soil stores carbon in the ground and prevents erosion.

In an effort to make guayule a more viable crop, researchers in academia and industry are working to increase the plant's rubber production—while also investigating uses for the sticky resin and woody material it produces. With guayule, "a farmer could still grow things in the desert and still make a living and still protect the soil and protect the water," says Catherine Brewer, a chemical engineer at New Mexico State University. "There are not many plants that meet all of those criteria."

The tire manufacturer Bridgestone has operated a demonstration-scale processing facility in central Arizona for the past decade in an effort to show that guayule can eventually be harvested for natural rubber at a commercial scale. In late August the company announced it would commercialize guayule rubber production by 2030. Though two thirds of the world's rubber is now made synthetically from petroleum, rubber produced from natural sources is indispensable for some purposes. Airplane tires, for example, are made from natural rubber, which is superior to synthetics for handling impacts such as landing on the runway.

Because only a small amount of guayule is currently grown, it wouldn't be able to compete with *Hevea* rubber on a broad scale for some time, says Katrina Cornish, who studies alternative rubber sources at the Ohio State University. That means companies that want to use it would need to start with high-value products—such as the guayule-rubber racing tire Bridgestone debuted this year. At her own company, EnergyEne, Cornish focuses on premium products made of guayule latex, a softer form of rubber that the plant also makes. EnergyEne is developing a radiation-attenuating medical glove, for example. On the consumer side, the company has made "lovely condoms," Cornish adds, including ones that are Cabernet Sauvignon- and Chardonnay-flavored. Guayule makes the best latex, compared with other natural and synthetic formulations, because it's particularly strong, stretchy and soft, Cornish says. It's also hypoallergenic, unlike latex derived from *Hevea* trees. Jason Quinn, a sustainability researcher at Colorado State University, conducted a study in 2020 that found that guayule rubber grown on a typical-size Arizona farm could be cost-competitive with *Hevea* rubber—though the guayule product's cost would be toward the higher end of the range of historical *Hevea* prices.

At Bridgestone, plant geneticist David Dierig hopes to improve guayule's profitability by breeding plants that bear more rubber. His team has mapped guayule's genome and identified genes that are associated with higher rubber content. With this information, researchers can select plants with a potential for greater rubber production and cross them before they are fully mature, shortening the time it would normally take to grow new generations. There is some limit to how much rubber any plant can produce, Dierig says, but it is hard to know where that limit is. He says that high-molecular-weight rubber—the kind used for tires—was initially around 2.8 percent of the plant, and he has brought it up to 3.8 percent. "We have to get rubber content to somewhere around 6 percent to be directly competitive [with *Hevea*]," Dierig says. Selling other products made from the plant's resin and woody parts, however, could help guayule be competitive before reaching that level of rubber, he adds.

The woody stems offer a less intensive option for developing guayule products to start to create more of a commercial incentive to cultivate the plant. In guayule processing, the bushes are ground up, and rubber and resin are extracted using a solvent, leaving behind a dry, sawdustlike material called bagasse. This can be pressed into particleboard such as the kind used in furniture or potentially made into biofuels for ships and planes—the latter conversion requires pyrolysis, a process in which the bagasse is heated in the absence of oxygen. "There's technology for that. It's feasible, but it costs a bit of energy," says Kim Ogden, who leads a U.S. Department of Agriculture–funded research project that is based at the University of Arizona and works with several partner institutions, including Bridgestone and Colorado State University. "So I'm not sure economically how great it is."

Ogden and other researchers think the real moneymaker could be guayule resin. The sticky substance is made up of many organic compounds, including essential oils that could be used as fragrances and other molecules called guayulins and argentatins that are unique to guayule. The researchers say the resin compounds hold promise for a number of potentially lucrative uses. Scientists at the University of Arizona found the resin could be used for plant-based adhesives, potentially replacing some formaldehyde-containing products such as wood glue. A recent study also found that argentatin-derived compounds were toxic toward three types of cancer cells, opening the possibility for their use in drug investigation.

New Mexico State University's Brewer leads a team that is testing whether the resin compounds could serve as insect repellents. She has designed experiments comparing cockroaches' responses to guayule resin extracts with their reactions to java oil (which is a known roach repellent) and acetone (which roaches don't mind). Some of the resin compounds, including some specific to guayule, thwarted roaches even more than the java oil—"which we thought was pretty exciting," she says. The insects appeared to dislike the scent of the resin, though more research is needed to understand how this possible repellent works. Brewer is also starting an experiment with mosquitoes. She thinks a guayule resin extract would likely repel them, too. But launching a topical consumer product requires a series of safety tests, and it is possible that these compounds might cause allergies or irritate skin.

"The resin has a huge mixture of compounds, and what's going to determine how it's used is how much money it takes to separate it, relative to the value of the products that you get," Brewer says. "So there's going to be some sweet spot of just enough processing and purification, compared to the uses, and we don't know where that sweet spot is yet."

Though guayule has a ways to go on the road to commercialization, the researchers involved are optimistic. Colorado State University's Quinn leads economic assessments for numerous emerging products and technologies—and he says only about one in 10 ends up seeming viable. "This," he says, "is one of those."

About the Author

Ula Chrobak is a freelance science journalist based in Reno, Nevada. You can read more of her work at her Web site: ulachrobak.com.

How Biotech Crops Can Crash— and Still Never Fail

By Aniket Aga and Maywa Montenegro De Wit

T he United Nations Food Systems Summit held in September 2020 was eclipsed by a powerful countermobilization effort led by farmers and scientists, as well as civil society groups allied with Indigenous communities and small-scale food producers across the world. These are the very people critical to achieving the summit's stated goals of ending hunger and promoting sustainable agriculture. The scientists and advocates accused summit organizers of compromising on food security, democratic accountability, sustainability, and the human rights of producers and workers in favor of transnational agribusinesses.

Opposition to the summit had been mounting since July, when hundreds of grassroots organizations challenged the organizers for framing the problem of food systems in narrow, technocratic ways and offering "false solutions" such as biotechnological interventions instead of promoting more sustainable, just and people-first ways of farming. Also in July the Philippines approved commercial cultivation of Bt eggplant, a genetically modified (GM) food that produces a protein that kills eggplant fruit and shoot borers, and "Golden Rice" altered to produce beta-carotene, the precursor of vitamin A. The Philippines thus became the first country in South and Southeast Asia to approve GM rice and the second in the world after Bangladesh to approve GM eggplant.

Advocates of GM crops hailed the Philippines' move as a triumph of science. Since the U.N.'s food summit was announced two years ago, different groups have steadily reduced applications of science to global problems to a limited set of investor-oriented innovations. Within this orbit, agricultural biotechnology and digitalization are touted as vital to achieving the U.N.'s sustainable development goals.

As governments now debate the way forward from the summit, it is critical to recognize that a narrow focus on technology to address the complex structural problems of farming and food has an astonishingly poor track record. In more than two decades of GM crops' cultivation, nearly every aspect of GM crop research, development and application has stoked scientific controversy.

At its base, GM crops are rooted in a colonial-capitalist model of agriculture based on theft of Indigenous land and on exploiting farmers' and food workers' labor, women's bodies, Indigenous knowledge and the web of life itself. The green revolution of the 1960s exported this paradigm to ex-colonial countries in South and Southeast Asia. Today this agricultural model is responsible not only for soaring farm debt, depleted soils, and threats to native seeds and biodiversity but also the erosion of farmers' knowledge and skills. The same model stands implicated in the emergence of novel pathogens and our increased vulnerability to pandemics. For the world to achieve sustainability, this colonial model of agriculture must be dismantled, and promising agroecological approaches premised on working with biodiversity and farmers' knowledge and skills should be brought center stage.

Maize and soy, along with cotton and canola, dominate the GM market. Most GM crops are engineered with resistance to herbicides and insects, which has not only contributed to the emergence of "superweeds" and soaring pesticide use but has driven the global consolidation of seed and chemical industries. These kinds of crops have principally benefited large-scale farmers, grain traders and multinational behemoths involved in selling seeds and pesticides.

Despite these problems, multinational agribusinesses have latched onto Golden Rice and Bt eggplant as ostensibly pro-poor technologies to win over smallholder farmers and consumers in the Global South. Since 2008 the International Rice Research Institute, based in the Philippines, has led Golden Rice's development with support from the Bill & Melinda Gates Foundation and in partnership with Syngenta (which owns rights to the rice) to address vitamin A deficiency (VAD) among the poor, especially children and pregnant women.

A crucial, unresolved question has been whether children can actually absorb beta-carotene from the rice. Its vitamin A content is low—relative to other, culturally more appropriate sources such as carrots and some leafy vegetables—and degrades with storage at room temperature, exposure to air and cooking.

The only available feeding study, published in 2009, had adult subjects eating Golden Rice, along with butter, oil, cashew nuts, meat and salad. More than 300 kilocalories came from fats, which aid the absorption of vitamin A. These conditions are hardly representative of poor, food-insecure households. Further, while efforts to introduce the trait into a local rice in Bangladesh have met with some success, in India, similar efforts resulted in a variety unsuitable for cultivation.

Such serious limitations would have derailed another project but not Golden Rice. In an exercise in grandstanding, more than 120 Nobel laureates endorsed an emotive appeal in 2016 supporting Golden Rice. This campaign involved figures such as a former Monsanto PR executive. Meanwhile studies by the Food and Nutrition Research Institute indicate marked success in combating vitamin A deficiency *without* any Golden Rice. Nutrition education, capsule supplements and other public programs in the Philippines have brought VAD down from a peak of 40.1 percent in 2003 to 15.5 percent in 2018–2019.

Bt eggplant was developed by the Indian company Mahyco, in which Monsanto held a 26 percent stake. It has stalled in India for more than a decade in part because of serious concerns of inducing antibiotic resistance in consumers, critically flawed toxicological analyses and threats to biodiversity. The same GMO has, however, been successfully marketed in Bangladesh and now the Philippines by actors linked to the Cornell Alliance for Science (a group backed by the Gates Foundation) and USAID. It is showcased as an innovation that will reduce both pesticide usage and losses from the eggplant fruit and shoot borer.

Yet research to support these claims tends to be both short-term and limited largely to monetary parameters. Bt cotton in India was marketed, starting in 2002, on the same twin planks of reduction in pesticide usage and losses from bollworms. Reviewing 18 years of experience, scientists found that pink bollworms became resistant to Bt cotton within a few years of large-scale adoption, forcing farmers to spray lethal amounts and fatal combinations of pesticides. The review concluded that Bt cotton's primary contribution to Indian agriculture was escalating pesticide use and costs of cultivation "rather than any enduring agronomic benefits."

GM crops have already saturated markets in corn, canola and soy in North and South America. For expansion, agribusiness is eyeing markets in lower-income countries and looking at smallholder crops, such as eggplant, millet and cassava. It is also assessing the use of gene editing as a tool to modify crop genomes.

It is therefore no surprise that the special envoy to the U.N. Food Systems Summit, Agnes Kalibata, was chosen from the Gates Foundation–sponsored Alliance for a Green Revolution in Africa. Nor is it surprising that after the U.N. entered into a strategic partnership with the World Economic Forum, summit science has come to mirror the forum's "fourth industrial revolution" approach to food systems change.

To connect investor-friendly tech innovations to the WEF's plank of free trade, the summit's leadership presents a simplistic picture of science—where technology innovates food systems without considerations of power and politics.

Yet decades of research has shown how biotechnology science is path-dependent, becoming more powerful as things such as patents make it increasingly lucrative for universities to do biotech research. More biotech research means more lab facilities, faculty and staff jobs, along with greater funding to support students who pursue this line of work. Over time, it has progressively become harder to conduct and publish research critical of GM crops. In effect, biotechnology has "locked out" other innovations, including agroecology.

Still, the case for agroecology grows stronger the more researchers learn. For instance, in 2009 a study comparing 840 MASIPAG farmers, part of a farmer-scientist network in the Philippines, found that 88 percent of agroecological adopters saw improvements in their food security, compared with 44 percent of nonadopters. Farmers who transitioned to agroecology ate 68 percent more vegetables, 56 percent more fruit, 55 percent more protein-rich staples and 40 percent more meat than before. New research by Debal Deb of the Center for Interdisciplinary Studies in India shows that mixed cropping patterns of Indigenous farmers in eastern India are significantly more productive than the single-cropping model of industrial farming.

Critics like to say these studies are cherry-picked. But the High Level Panel of Experts in 2019 took this challenge on. Its results show that agroecology has received much less investment in R&D than ecofriendly spins on the dominant technocratic approaches. Yet agroecology continues to generate ecological and social gains across scales, particularly when formal research institutions recognize the expertise of social movements and when women's rights are central. Biodiversity-rich farms with complex relationships among multiple species are also more resilient and sustainable. A new meta-analysis of two decades of research found that agroecological practices improve nutrition and food security outcomes in low- and middle-income countries—and the more practices farmers included, the greater the benefits.

To say that smallholder and Indigenous agroecologists are experts in their own right is not to say things are fine for them. COVID-19 brought preexisting vulnerabilities and inequalities into sharp relief. It highlighted that a food system based on global supply chains, market-led food provision and export orientation—exactly the approach promoted by the U.N. Food Systems Summit—is brittle and prone to crisis. Rather than celebrate grossly inadequate and unscientific solutions, the global community must support what hundreds of millions of agriculturalists represented by the Civil Society and Indigenous Peoples Mechanism are asking for: robust international support for agroecology within a governing framework of human rights, peasant rights, and food sovereignty.

About the Authors

Aniket Aga teaches environmental studies and anthropology at Krea University in India. He is the author of Genetically Modified Democracy: Transgenic Crops in Contemporary India, *published by Yale University Press.*

Maywa Montenegro De Wit is an assistant professor in the department of environmental studies at the University of California, Santa Cruz. Combining theories and methods from political ecology, science and technology studies, and agroecology, she studies knowledge politics in struggles for just and sustainable food systems

GLOSSARY

agroecology A way of producing food that imitates natural biological processes, relying on biological diversity and the recycling of natural resources and nutrients.

algorithm A series of steps taken to solve a mathematical problem or accomplish a task in software.

biodiversity A measure of the variety of interdependent life-forms in an existing environment.

biotechnology The use of engineering to manipulate life-forms to create products and services that improve health or increase agricultural production.

energy transition Historical shift in the use of energy sources from fossil fuels such as oil and natural gas to renewable energy such as solar panels and wind turbines.

environmental justice A movement that seeks to correct unequal exposure to pollution, hazardous wastes, and the effects of climate change to women and poor or marginalized people.

greenhouse gas One of a number of gases, such as carbon dioxide (CO_2), methane (CH_4), and nitrous oxide (N_2O), that trap heat in the atmosphere and contribute to increases in global temperatures.

Green Revolution A period of agricultural changes beginning in the 1940s characterized by the use of new breeds of crops and chemically engineered fertilizers and pesticides to increase food production.

machine learning A key feature of artificial intelligence whereby software is able to analyze data and perform new tasks without being explicitly programmed to do so.

FURTHER INFORMATION

Berkowitz, Rachel. "Ultrasound Enables Remote 3-D Printing—Even in the Human Body," *Scientific American*, December 11, 2023, https://www.scientificamerican.com/article/ultrasound-enables-remote-3-d-printing-even-in-the-human-body/.

Braxton Little, Jane. "AI Could Spot Wildfires Faster Than Humans," *Scientific American*, June 17, 2021, https://www.scientificamerican.com/article/ai-could-spot-wildfires-faster-than-humans/.

The Editors of *Scientific American*. "Changing Car Culture Can Benefit Our Health and Our Planet," *Scientific American*, March 1, 2024, https://www.scientificamerican.com/article/changing-car-culture-can-benefit-our-health-and-our-planet/.

Hafner, Katie, and Carol Sutton Lewis. "The First Lady of Engineering," *Scientific American*, September 22, 2023, https://www.scientificamerican.com/article/the-first-lady-of-engineering-lost-women-of-science-podcast-season-3-episode-1/.

Langer, Robert, and Nicholas A. Peppas. "A Bright Future in Medicine for Chemical Engineering," *Nature*, January 11, 2024, https://www.nature.com/articles/s44286-023-00016-y.

Thompson, Andrea. "Here's How Much Food Contributes to Climate Change," *Scientific American*, September 13, 2021, https://www.scientificamerican.com/article/heres-how-much-food-contributes-to-climate-change/.

Willingham, Emily. "New Brain Implant Transmits Full Words from Neural Signals," *Scientific American*, July 15, 2021, https://www.scientificamerican.com/article/new-brain-implant-transmits-full-words-from-neural-signals/.

CITATIONS

1.1 Entire Buildings Can Be Wrapped in Jackets to Save Energy by Willem Marx (July 29, 2021); 1.2 New Air-Conditioning Technology Could Be the Future of Cool by Lauren Leffer (August 29, 2023); 1.3 Recycled Wind Turbines Could Be Made into Plexiglass, Diapers or Gummy Bears by Sophie Bushwick (August 26, 2022); 1.4 New Space Station Sensor Can Reveal Hidden Greenhouse Gas Polluters by Meghan Bartels (November 17, 2023); 1.5 Pipelines Touted as Carbon Capture Solution Spark Uncertainty and Opposition by Anna Mattson (October 1, 2023); 1.6 How to Make Urban Agriculture More Climate-Friendly by Joanna Thompson (February 2, 2024); 1.7 Don't Fall for Big Oil's Carbon Capture Deceptions by Jonathan Foley (December 4, 2023); 2.1 Millions of Mosquitoes Will Rain Down on Hawaii to Save an Iconic Bird by Sarah Wild (October 6, 2023); 2.2 Tiny 'Rover' Explores Cells without Harming Them by Andrew Chapman (November 21, 2022); 2.3 Tiny, Tumbling Origami Robots Could Help with Targeted Drug Delivery by Fionna M. D. Samuels (June 14, 2022); 2.4 This Sticker Looks Inside the Body by Sophie Bushwick (July 29, 2022); 2.5 Why Is It So Hard to Make Vegan Fish? by Joanna Thompson (February 28, 2023); 2.6 Synthetic Enamel Could Make Teeth Stronger and Smarter by Joanna Thompson (February 4, 2022); 2.7 Soft Robot Hand Is First to Be Fully 3-D-Printed in a Single Step by Sophie Bushwick (July 23, 2021); 3.1 Drones Could Spot Crime Scenes from Afar by Rachel Berkowitz (May 1, 2022); 3.2 Firefighting Robots Go Autonomous by Jane Braxton Little (October 29, 2021); 3.3 The NYPD's Robot Dog Was a Really Bad Idea by Sophie Bushwick (May 7, 2021); 3.4 AIs Spot Drones with Help from a Fly Eye by Monique Brouillette (April 20, 2022); 3.5 AI Creates False Documents That Fake Out Hackers by Sophie Bushwick (July 1, 2021); 3.6 AI's Climate Impact Goes beyond Its Emissions by Jude Coleman (December 7, 2023); 3.7 Elon Musk's Neuralink Has Implanted Its First Chip in a Human Brain by Ben Guarino (January 30, 2024); 4.1 Future Space Travel Might Require Mushrooms by Nick Hilden (August 3, 2021); 4.2 Rotating Sails Help to Revive Wind-Powered Shipping by Lynn Freehill-Maye (December 1, 2020); 4.3 Will Trackless Trams Gain Traction in the U.S. by Sophie Bushwick (March 1, 2021); 4.4 Better Bus Systems Could Slow Climate Change by Kendra Pierre-Louis (May 1, 2023); 4.5 Access to Electric Vehicles Is an Environmental Justice Issue by Neha Palmer (November 2, 2021); 5.1 Farm Protests in India Are Writing the Green Revolution's Obituary by Aniket Aga (January 24, 2021); 5.2 Agroecology Is the Solution to World Hunger by Raj Patel (September 22, 2021); 5.3 Designer Crops of the Future Must Be Better Tailored for Women in Agriculture by Vivian Polar and Matty Demont (July 25, 2022); 5.4 The Future of Fish Farming May Be Indoors by Laura Poppick (September 17, 2018); 5.5 Robotic Bees Could Support Vertical Farms Today and Astronauts Tomorrow by Molly Glick (July 17, 2023); 5.6 Lab-Grown Meat Approved for Sale: What You Need to Know by Joanna Thompson (June 30, 2023); 5.7 This Shrub Could Supply Rubber, Insect Repellent and Glue by Ula Chrobak (October 14, 2022); 5.8 How Biotech Crops Can Crash—and Still Never Fail by Aniket Aga and Maywa Montenegro De Wit (December 27, 2021)

Each author biography was accurate at the time the article was originally published.

INDEX